SONG TITLE SERIES

FIVE
COUNTRY MEN

FEATURING

LEE KERNAGHAN

ADAM HARVEY

TROY CASSAR-DALEY

JAMES BLUNDELL

ADAM BRAND

JOAN MAGUIRE

Copyright Page

New: Five Country Men

Author: Joan Maguire

National Library of Australia Cataloguing-in-Publication – Publication entry

Author:	Maguire, Joan.
Title:	Five Country Men / Joan Maguire.
ISBN:	9780980855166
Series:	Song title series.
Subjects:	Country musician --Biography
	Five Country Men (Country Singers)
	Australian Country Singers—Australia--Biography
	Country Singers—Australia--Biography

Dewey Number: 781.642092

Published with the assistance of Love of Books and is available through the Print on Demand network and www.songtitleseries.com

The original short story book was created and written by
Joan Maguire on 28th December 2010 ©
ISBN 978-0-9808551-6-6

E-book re-written April 2014©and is available on
www.songtitleseries.com
EIBSN: 978-0-9925964-3-9

The large print book was created in March 2015© and is available
through the same distributors as the normal book or
www.songtitleseries.com
ISBN .978-0-9943297-2-1 (large print)

DEDICATION

I would like to dedicate this book and say to thank you to my Earth Angel David and his friends, who inspire and motivate me to achieve things that I never dreamt, were possible.

INTRODUCTION

This time my challenge was to write five different stories, using five Australian country male singers. It was hard to choose from so many Australian male country singers so I chose Lee Kernaghan, Adam Harvey, Troy Cassar-Daley, James Blundell and Adam Brand as their songs and their styles in writing were all different.

Legally I can not use Lyrics or Music because of Copyright but I can use song titles (Italicized) and due to the nature of my books; legally I must place a Reference (exactly as it is down loaded) and Bibliography after the story

For each of the artists, I have written their own little book which includes a Reference and Bibliography at the end of their story. Each artist's management kindly supplied the picture to introduce that particular artist's story.

When reading this "Song Title Series" book, I hope that no disservice has been done to the band as well as their adoring fans who read it, for that was not my intention. As I may have missed a song, an album or a concert within this book I do apologize sincerely.

So, sit back, relax and enjoy reading these short stories and don't forget; because I have used the original song titles in whole, there are places in the book that I could not change to make it more comprehensible for you the reader.

ACKNOWLEDGEMENTS

I would like to thank my daughters, Jenny and Kylie for their positive but critical input in the first draft of this book and all the help and support that they have given me throughout the Song Title Series books. With taking their input to mind, I have improved the book.

I would also like to thank my son Peter and his family for their support and help in keeping me grounded.

I would like to say a special thank you to my brother Colin and his wife Beth who have given me so much help in authenticating parts of this story.

I would like to thank the artists and their management for supplying the pictures to introduce their stories.

I would like to thank Kay and Julie for their patience and understanding whilst teaching me and giving me the skills to present my unique books in the best way possible.

I would also like to thank Phat (Pat) for his help with the translation in the Adam Brand story.

And thank you to everyone else who has helped me bring this book to life and to you for purchasing it.

OTHER BOOKS IN THE SONG TITLE SERIES

CONTENTS

LEE KERNAGHAN

TALLAROOK'S JOURNEY

Looking out of the *Darwin Jailhouse window, Tallarook,* the *Tenterfield saddler,* started *following the light* of the first truck in a road train leaving the city for another part of this beautiful *planet country* of Australia.

He thought to himself "What am I doing here in this cell? I should be back in *Texas Qld 4385* with the *boys from the bush,* following the *family tradition* of mustering horses through the *dirt* and dust of this dry outback country.

Once we'd reach *Kerosene Lane,* the *cowgirl* in charge would tell us where to take the lead horse; would we take it to *the old block* behind the shed or would we *leave him in the longyard* for the night.

We all know out here that *the spirit of the bush* is only one reason that helps the families through the good and the bad times and *love in the time of drought* is another reason. When I'm home, *I milk cows* in the early morning and do other station hand work till sundown.

I wish I could remember what happened the other day. I remember talking with one of the *boys from the bush* who was with some other fella; although, I don't think that he was an *Australian boy.* I think that he came in with the *boys from Bathurst,* but with the *country crowd* that was in the *Hat Town* Hotel that night, it would've been hard to tell.

I remember he got *rejected* by some *country girls* from the *Collingullie Station* in wanting to dance the *Christmas waltz* with him; therefore, it *must be Christmas. When country comes* to town to have a *merry Christmas,* they usually do.

As the *country's really big these days,* the *boys from the bush* enjoy having a few days off to enjoy themselves *on the beach* and especially the surf. Most of the year, the *boys from the bush* are either droving cattle, station hands or they go out and *baptise the Ute, scrubbashin',* while trying to disperse packs of wild dingoes or wild pigs.

Where I come from, *Texas Qld 4385,* yes; *I'm from the country; the boys from the bush, the outback club,* would usually go *skinny dippin'* after a hard day and before they gathered *by a fire of gidgee coal* to eat the meal that the cook had prepared for them and they would *pass the bottle round,* usually there was more than one bottle being handed around.

3

Many *long nights* were spent this way when they were out droving and only having the *bare essentials* with them, the boys would often sleep under the *Goondiwindi moon* and stars. During summer, living like that was great but when the *winter winds* blew strong in the *high country, where the whitefaced cattle roam,* any sort of *shelter* that you could find was great.

I remember back in *1959* when *I was only nineteen,* yep; they were the *days of old Khancoban.* He was such a high spirited colt, and after he had broken out of the stable and took off, we had to chase him down to bring him back down from the *high country.* The boss told the *Cunnamulla fella* to *leave him in the longyard* as he was going to the *Electric Rodeo* the following day, for one of the *Scots of the Riverina* to ride.

The boss asked me what I was up to that evening and I told him that I might be going *scrubbashin'* with Betsy.

He then asked me if she was a *cowgirl* from a neighbouring property and I replied "Nah, *she's my Ute* and *she waits by the sliprails* for me."

I told him that sometimes I drive her out to the dam, go *skinny dippin'* and then *listen to the radio* while I dry off by a small *fire.*

I remember the boss telling me to be careful as there could be *something in the water* of the dam that can make *an ordinary bloke* see *little men* that look *like angels.*

He told me that a couple of years back, a *Cunnamulla fella* found *Janine walking out west* of the dam wearing a strange kind of hat, smiling and talking about the blue eyed guy with the cutest smile. She said he looked like an angel and he was supposed to have said to her *"You don't have to go to Memphis* to get *the western beat. Livin' in Australia* is a great place to live. *This is the outback* where the sun is so hot, that it burns *the rope that pulls the wind* so you must wear *this cowboy's hat* that I am giving to you now, whenever you are outside.

He also told her that under a *Goondiwindi moon,* someone will *sing you back home to me."*

The boss then said that he'd believe in what she said about angels *when the snow falls on the Alice* and there ain't no likely hood of that seeing where Alice Spring lies.

Later that year in *1959,* when I was in *Camooweal* for their *Electric Rodeo,* the *southern son* of a family from *Lonlyville,* who was playing in the band *Getting' Gone,* said that they passed an unusual looking bloke on the *Three Chain Road.* When they reached the *Three Rivers Hotel,* there was the same guy walking out of *The Outback Club,* carrying *Mary's boy child.* He said that the band members watched him walk down under a bridge and disappear but they still couldn't understand how he could have got to their destination on foot before they drove in.

Getting' Gone played their gig that night after day one of the *Electric Rodeo* and they played the next two nights; then *Getting' Gone* just broke up before finishing the rest of their booking.

One member went *gold* digging in *Australia's western world,* two members went to the *wild side of life* in Sydney and the *southern son* became a *Diamantina drover.*"

Tallarook's thoughts were broken by the excited voice of a little girl shouting out "*Santa Claus is back in town.*" and with other people calling out to one another "*We wish you a merry Christmas.*" or "*Have yourself a merry little Christmas.*" and he could just see the road in front of a church, from where he was standing.

He could just make out the top of the Nativity scene where taped music played *O' Little Town Of Bethlehem* and *Away In A Manger,* a couple of times a day. Then he heard the carol *Silent Night,* that made him look over towards the church and he could clearly see a fair haired man, standing and smiling at him.

Then in his head, he heard "You will not be the *talk of the town* nor will this leave any *scars. The way it is* now, will not remain so. You will not have the *Aussie doghouse blues* for much longer. A *girl's gone wild* and hasn't stopped talking down at the *Hat Town* Hotel and *Congaro Chigago* will find out *something right* in what she has said.

There are only *a few of us* left and we know that a *bushman can't survive* without a *mate,* the *spirit of the bush* or the *spirit of the high country.*

In a few days, *when the snow falls on the Alice,* you will once again walk *the Overlander Trail,* where you will enjoy *the burning heart* of the land and the cool evenings under the *western stars,* for that's *where country is* and where you belong.

The *southern son* who became a *Diamantina drover* did see me, as *that's the kinda life I live* in your world."

Tallarook blinked and saw that the man had gone; he had just disappeared. It reminded him of Janine's story that the boss had told him, as well as the snow remark.

"What did that voice in my head mean when he said "*The way it is* for me right now?" Am I seeing and hearing things?

If I am in for a *blue Christmas,* this cell is *a place for me* to spend it in.

This is frustrating me, if only I could remember what happened in the *Hat Town* Hotel that evening." he thought.

There was a noise outside his cell and the door unlocked.

A gentleman, who looked like a lawyer, walked in and said "Tallarook, you are free to go. You were not charged for any crime; however, under the circumstances of the trouble at the time and your memory loss, we had no other choice but to hold you for forty eight hours.

When you were first brought in here, a doctor was called to attend to you. He did some test and found that there was something *in the water* of *the glass on the bar* that you last drank from. It had an unidentifiable drug in it and we believe that the same thing happened at the *Hat Town* Hotel and *The Odyssey* Hotel around this time last year.

Last night at the *Hat Town* Hotel, a *Cunnamulla fella,* named *Changi Bango* was caught by some *country girls,* trying to slip *something in the water* that they were drinking and complained to the management who called the police.

The police questioned him and he eventually confessed to spiking the water so that the girls would spend time with him. He saw you and thought that you had seen him spiking the water jugs, so he spiked your drink to keep you quiet.

I want to thank you because *you're the reason I never saw Hank Jr play* his violin and he's terrible at playing it. *I'm from the country* and the *country's really big these days,* but not big enough for my grandson's violin playing.

You should be as good as *gold* by later this afternoon. Now, where will you go when you leave here?"

"I think I'll make my way *back to the shack* near *Sassafras Gap*, to Betsy." said Tallarook.

"Betsy. Your girlfriend I suppose. I bet your shack will become a *love shack* when you get home?" said the gentleman.

Tallarook laughed and said "Betsy, *she's my Ute* and *she waits by the sliprails* for me. *It still feels like Christmas to me,* so I think that I'll hitch *that old caravan* to the Ute and take off home to *Texas Qld 4385.*

I have to tell you this; just before you came in and told me the good news, I was standing looking out the window towards the church and I saw this fair haired bloke clearly, like you are to me, and I heard a voice in my head. Some things I heard I understood but other bits, I didn't."

"*When country comes* to this town, the *boys from the bush* bring *The Outback Club* and other people with them. Sometimes a local *girls gone wild* over one of the boys but the boys do *something right* by discouraging the girls. They fear that the girls could become uncontrollable *great balls of fire* and that would prevent the boys coming back to town again.

Every now and then, a feller, they call Earth Angel David, comes with them to help someone in need. It seems that you were very lucky because he has helped you and now he is *searchin' for another you* to help.

The way it is with *people like us, a bushman can't survive* without a mate, a *spirit of the bush* or a *spirit of the high country,* but today, he became all three of them for you.

Well, you had better be off if you want to get home for Christmas. You know the *rules of the road* so don't go speeding but if you go down *Three Chain Road,* it will take you straight to *Freedom Road.* From that road, you can go anywhere you want to go in this *planet country,* to the *high country* or to *Longreach* or back home.

If I were you, I'd be *losin' my blues tonight* with the *boys from the bush* over at the *Cobar Line* Hotel just so that you will be right as rain to drive safely tomorrow.

The *cowgirls do* come as *close as a whisper* under a *Goondiwindi moon* especially if they are at the *Watermelon Bowling* Lanes, outback in *the old block* of the hotel.

They may even try to get you *feeling pretty naked* when they want you to go *skinny dippin'* with them in the dam next to the hotel; however, you are not like the *boys from the bush* and you most probably have that *Diamantina dream* of settling down one day.

Love in the time of drought may not work for everyone and *love hurts* and leaves *scars* when it goes wrong for everyone, not just for *people like us.*" said the gentleman.

Tallarook replied "Once I'm out of here, I'll be following that *Three Chain Road* till I get to Betsy. Don't forget that *I'm from the country too* and I know how *love hurts.*

Betsy, *she's my Ute* and she doesn't care if there is *dust on my boots* when I get in her, or if I drive her on *dirt* roads. I just get in her and drive to wherever I want to *in my outback world* and that's *the kind of life I live* and that's *the way it is* for me."

"Well." said the gentleman "you have a safe trip to wherever you're going. *I'll remember you* tomorrow around lunchtime 'cos it's when I've finished my work at home. *I milk cows* first up in the mornings, then take the pony down and *leave him in the longyard,* so he can graze on *the new bush,* make *Rachel's bed* and listen again to her singing version of *Great Balls Of Fire* and *You Rock My World.*

My daughter is still too young to go to *The Outback Club,* and because she's *still missing Slim,* I have to put up with her *bringing home the music.* Me, I hate listening to her music *cause I'm country* through and through and so was my wife.

Go on, get going. I know how quick you want to leave here so grab *the bare essentials* you'll need to take and *baptise the Ute* with a *handful of dust* under the *Goondiwindi moon.* Good luck and have a happy Christmas and a good new year."

Tallarook said "You too. Let's *shake on it.* The way it's looking now, I hope that *in my next life,* I can be a cat that just lazes around all day, gets fed and made a fuss of. Now that's what I call a good life."

REFERENCE

1959
SCRUBBASHIN'
JANINE
SHAKE ON IT LYRICS
COUNTRY CROWD
DOCTOR
RACHEL'S BED
WHERE COUNTRY IS
FREDOM ROAD
SKINNY DIPPIN' LYRICS
THIS COWBOY'S HAT
THE ROPE THAT PULLS THE WIND
1959

ELECTRIC RODEO
THE WAY IT IS LYRICS
ELECTRIC RODEO LYRICS
SOMETHING IN THE WATER LYRICS
AN ORDINARY BLOKE LYRICS
BAPTISE THE UTE LYRICS
LONG NIGHT LYRICS
YOU ROCK MY WORLD
A HANDFUL OF DUST
THAT OLD CARAVAN LYRICS
WILD SIDE OF LIFE LYRICS
SING YOU BACK HOME TO ME LYRICS
TEXAS QLD 4385
THE ODYSSEY LYRICS

ELECTRIC RODEO 2
I'M FROM THE COUNTRY LYRICS
SPIRIT OF THE HIGH COUNTRY
LOVE HURTS (WITH CATHERINE BRITT)
CONGARO CHIGAGO
IN MY NEXT LIFE
THIS IS THE OUTBACK
MATE
DIAMANTINA DROVER LYRICS
BOYS FROM BATHURST LYRICS
GREAT BALLS OF FIRE

HAT TOWN
HAT TOWN LYRICS
BARE ESSENTIALS
GOONDIWINDI MOON
A FEW OF US LEFT
WHEN THE SNOW FALLS ON THE ALICE
CHANGI BANGO
COWGIRLS DO
GETTIN' GONE
PASS THE BOTTLE ROUND
THE WESTERN BEAT
LONGREACH
LONLYVILLE

RULES OF THE ROAD
LOSIN' MY BLUES TONIGHT LYRICS
DARWIN JAILHOUSE WINDOW LYRICS
RULES OF THE ROAD
CUNNAMMULLA FELLA
THAT'S THE KINDA LIFE I LIVE
WHERE THE WHITEFACED CATTLE ROAM
THE GLASS ON THE BAR
WINTER WINDS
AUSSIE DOGHOUSE BLUES
BY A FIRE OF GIDGEE COAL
THE OVERLANDER TRAIL
CAMOOWEAL
FOLLOWING THE LIGHT
A BUSHMAN CAN'T SURVIVE LYRICS
DAYS OF OLD KHANACOBAN
LEAVE HIM IN THE LONGYARD

BIG ONES
HAT TOWN LYRICS
BOTS FROM THE BUSH LYRICS
SOMETHING IN THE WATER LYRICS
GOONDIWINDI MOON
THE WAY IT IS LYRICS
LEAVE HIM IN THE LONGYARD
SHE'S MY UTE
WHEN THE SNOW FALLS ON THE ALICE
HIGH COUNTRY
SKINNY DIPPIN' LYRICS

1959
GETTIN' GONE LYRICS
I'M FROM THE COUNTRY LYRICS
THREE CHAIN ROAD LYRICS
SHE WAITS BY THE SLIPRAILS
TEXAS QLD 4385 LYRICS
ELECTRIC RODEO
THE OUTBACK CLUB LYRICS
MISSIN' SLIM (WITH COLLIN BUCHANAN) LYRICS
DOWN UNDER

THE OUTBACK CLUB
BOYS FROM THE BUSH LYRICS
HIGH COUNTRY
SHE WAITS BY THE SLIPRAILS (THE BUSH GIRL)
WALKIN' OUT WEST
COUNTRY GIRLS
COUNTRY'S REALLY BIG THESE DAYS
YOU'RE THE REASON I NEVER SAW HANK JR PLAY
REJECTED
SCOTS OF THE RIVERINA
YOU DON'T HAVE TO GO TO MEMPHIS
SEARCHIN' FOR ANOTHER YOU
TALLAROOK

THREE CHAIN ROAD
THE OUTBACK CLUB LYRICS
THREE CHAIN ROAD LYRICS
SHE'S MY UTE
DUST ON MY BOOTS
THE BURNING HEART
'CAUSE I'M COUNTRY
COLLINGULLIE STATION LYRICS
LEAVE HIM IN THE LONGYARD (WITH SLIM DUSTY)
SOUTHERN SON
BACK TO THE SHACK
COBAR LINE
WESTERN STARS

THE CHRISTMAS ALBUM
SANTA CLAUS IS BACK IN TOWN
IT MUST BE CHRISTMAS
MARY'S BOY CHILD

MERRY MERRY CHRISTMAS
CHRISTMAS WALTZ
HAVE YOURSELF A MERRY LITTLE CHRISTMAS
BLUE CHRISTMAS
IT STILL FEELS LIKE CHRISTMASTIME TO ME
O' LITTLE TOWN OF BETHLEHEM
SILENT NIGHT
WE WISH YOU A MERRY CHRISTMAS
AWAY IN A MANGER

THE NEW BUSH
WHERE I COME FROM
LISTEN TO THE RADIO
THE NEW BUSH
DIAMANTINA DREAM
LOVE SHACK
WESTERN WORLD
I'LL REMEMBER YOU
LIVIN' IN AUSTRALIA
LITTLE MEN
LIKE ANGELS
ON THE BEACH
WHEN COUNTRY COMES
CLOSE AS A WHISPER (THE GIFT)

SPIRIT OF THE BUSH
SASSAFRAS GAP
I WAS ONLY NINETEEN (A WALK IN THE LIGHT GREEN)
THREE RIVERS HOTEL
SPIRIT OF THE BUSH
DIAMANTINA DROVER
BARE ESSENTIALS
THE WAY IT IS
SPIRIT OF THE HIGH COUNTRY
SOUTHERN SON
SHELTER
WHEN COUNTRY COMES
A BUSHMAN CAN'T SURVIVE
MATE
TENTERFIELD SADDLER
CUNNAMULLA FELLER
HAT TOWN
SPIRIT OF THE BUSH (REPRISE)

PLANET COUNTRY
PLANET COUNTRY
LOVE IN THE TIME OF DROUGHT
PEOPLE LIKE US
DIRT
GOLD
SCARS
SOMETHING RIGHT
COWGIRL
OLD BLOCK, THE
AUSTRALIAN BOY
GIRLS GONE WILD
A PLACE FOR ME (PLANET COUNTRY REPRISE)
I MILK COWS
BRINGING HOME THE MUSIC (PUBS,
CLUBS AND CARPARKS TOUR THEME)
FIRE
FEELING PRETTY NAKED
KEROSENE LANE
MY OUTBACK WORLD (OPENING THEME:
RM WILLIAMS OUTBACK SPECTACULAR)
GREAT BALLS OF FIRE (LIVE AT CMC ROCKS THE SNOWYS)
SPIRIT OF THE BUSH (LIVE AT CMC ROCKS THE SNOWYS)
TALK OF THE TOWN
FAMILY TRADITION
TEXAS QLD 4385 (LIVE AT CMC ROCKS THE SNOWYS)

PLANET COUNTRY CD TRACK LISTING 2009
PLANET COUNTRY
LOVE IN THE TIME OF DROUGHT
PEOPLE LIKE US
DIRT
GOLD
SCARS
SOMETHING RIGHT
COWGIRL
OLD BLOCK, THE
AUSTRALIAN BOY
GIRL'S GONE WILD
PLACE FOR ME, A (PLANET COUNTRY REPRISE)
I MILK COWS

13

LEE KERNAGHAN – ACCESS ALL AREAS DVD
THE WAY IT IS
SOMETHING IN THE WATER
COUNTRY'S REALLY BIG THESE DAYS
HAT TOWN
I'M FROM THE COUNTRY
SCRUBBASHIN'
BOYS FROM THE BUSH
HIGH COUNTRY
SOUTHERN SONS
GETTIN' GONE
GOONDIWINDI MOON
CUNNAMULLA FELLA
THAT'S THE KIND OF LIFE I LIVE
THE WAY IT IS
LOVE HURTS
THE OUTBACK CLUB (LIVE)
BOYS FROM THE BUSH (LIVE)
COUNTRY GIRLS (LIVE)
WATERMELON BOWLING
BOYS FROM THE BUSH
THREE CHAIN ROAD
BOYS FROM THE BUSH
GOONDIWINDI MOON
BAPTISE THE UTE
OUTBACK CLUB
BOYS FROM THE BUSH
SHE'S MY UTE (BURKE'S BACKYARD SHOW) SKINNY DIPPIN'
HAT TOWN (TOYOTA MUSTER)
ELECTRIC RODEO (CLOSING CREDITS)

BIBLIOGRAPHY

Lee Kernaghan picture: Courtesy Stephen White Management

THE FOLLOWING ALBUMS WERE FOUND AT:
http://artists.letssingit.com/lee-kernaghan-rzr6v/albums
      1959
      ELECTRIC RODEO
      ELECTRIC RODEO 2
      HAT TOWN
      RULES OF THE ROAD
      THE BIG ONES VOLUME 1
      THE OUTBACK CLUB
      THREE CHAIN ROAD

THE FOLLOWING ALBUMS WERE FOUND AT:
http://www.leekernaghan.com.au/music/
      THE CHRISTMAS ALBUM
      THE NEW BUSH
      SPITIR OF THE BUSH
      PLANET COUNTRY

PLANET COUNTRY CD TRACK LISTING:
http://www.cduniverse.com/productinfo.asp?pid=8308270

LEE KERNAGHAN – ACCESS ALL AREAS DVD:
http://www.gumtreemusic.com.au/music/lee-kernaghan/access-all-areas.aspx

ADAM HARVEY

THE MYSTERIOUS TRUCKER

Mr. Bojangles wrote in his letter to the *Gypsy Queen,* "I'm sitting *in the jailhouse now,* waiting for *Jackson,* my lawyer, to bring me an update on the investigation that's going on. He has been *working overtime* on my case, but no one really knows what really happened to the *seven Spanish angels* who were singing along with the band *Missing Heroes.*

You know me; remember when we had our last *Louisiana rendezvous* and all those *trashy women* that I left with *Cadillac tears, sad song and waltzes* unfinished; well, something happened to me once I started travelling through the outback of Australia.

I was hitch hiking from Mt Isa to Tenant Creek, where I could continue south to Alice Springs or go north to Darwin, when a road train pulled up beside me. The driver opened the passenger side door and said "I'm the *King of the road* and this 'ere truck is the *Phantom 309.* If you want a lift down aways, then jump in."

It was so hot walking that I decided to climb into the cabin of the truck where it was cooler and the driver looked at me, smiled and said "Riding with me is going to be a whole lot better than being *stuck in the middle* of two towns with no food, water or shelter for days. Even *old dogs and children and watermelon wine* wouldn't last too long out here in this heat."

Then from the sleeping section of the truck's cabin, I heard a low growl.

"*Hush.*" said the driver "*move it on over* and *Lady lay down.*"

Then the driver continued saying "Lady's my dog. *Once upon a long time ago,* I was driving this road, when someone in a blue Holden Ute overtook me and as they were driving *way too fast,* they didn't see the mother dog or her pup on the side of the road. They swerved to miss a pot hole and hit the mother, killing her instantly and left the pup injured. I stopped and adopted the little *orphan of the road* and she's been with me ever since.

If we see a hitch hiker *stuck in the middle* of nowhere, I'll stop and pick them up unless Lady barks as we approach. She's *one of a kind* and one day her barking saved me from being *the biggest fool* ever.

The police notified all truckers on their radios about a dangerous escapee, who was dressed in grey overalls, had shaggy shoulder length black hair and was carrying a stolen green backpack. They said that he was heading for Western Australia via the outback and one *Saturday night,* I was going to pick up this guy on a deserted stretch of track, when Lady really went off her rocker, barking and growling and I realized that this guy was the escapee, so I kept going but notified the cops of his whereabouts.

Lady saved me from maybe getting killed. Now; *that's what you call a friend* and the escapee was recaptured two days later."

Lady poked her head out of the sleeping section and the driver said as he patted her on the head *"Hello darlin',* you ready for a break and a run? Your favourite place The *Sugar Talk* Roadhouse is just up the road."

The driver glanced at me and said "What's your name, stranger?"

I told him that my name was *Mr. Bojangles,* but most people call me Bo."

"Well Bo." he said "you are quite welcome to stay with us until we reach Tenant Creek."

I asked the driver his name and he looked at me with these unforgettable blue eyes, grinned and said "I'm known as the *King of the road* but *where I come from,* they just call me King."

We pulled into a busy roadhouse and the King disappeared out back for a while, leaving me to have something to eat and drink and when he returned, he was wearing blue *tight fittin' jeans* and a black fitted tee shirt, very much unlike a truck driver would wear.

The other truck drivers never took any notice of King; it was as if they never saw him come into the roadhouse or even walk past them.

I realized that in some way, King was very different from most other men I had met, yet I couldn't figure out in what way he was different. I don't know if he had anything to eat or not whilst he was gone.

In the roadhouse, where most of the truckies were, there were some country scene pictures and four sayings hanging on the *walls.*

One sign said *"God made beer,* so that's *good enough for me* to drink it."

Another said "The *Genie in the bottle* will have you *acting a little crazy* if you drink too much."

After a good break playing with Lady, I joined King on the road.

The King broke the silence by saying "*Life don't have to mean nothin' at all.* A *little cowboy dreams* of being a big *cowboy for a day* and even owning his own property.

The older I get, I find that the *little bitty thing called love* can be a *little unfair,* especially when the *love bug* bites you with just *the shake of a hand. I'm doin' alright* 'cos *I've been loved by the best* and even though *it's all over now,* I've become *a better man* because of it."

I looked out the side window before saying "You're lucky because I've had nothing but *bad luck with women. When lonely met love,* for me, it was in the form of *Cheryl Moana Marie,* a very beautiful woman. She was very *easy* to love and I used to send her *flowers* about twice a week.

One evening, while we were out on the veranda of *the house that Jack built,* her brother's house, I asked her "*Will you be mine?*" and her reply was "Yes, I will. You know that I have to be up early tomorrow, so I had better be getting inside. *Goodnight sweetheart.*"

When I went to see her the following evening, *she was gone, gone, gone,* but she did leave a note with her brother that read "Bo, I'm sorry. *I'm sick and tired of you* sending me *flowers* twice a week. I know that *when you love somebody,* you want to be with them, only I want to be with *big bad John,* who has many *boats to build* and test at sea.

He has *a bigger plan* for his life and I know that he will not *treat me like a dog* either. I have been *stuck in the middle* between both of you. Last night, I had to make a choice and say goodbye to one of you. My feeling towards you is not *what it used to be,* but John, *he lives my dream.*

This decision has not been *easy* for me to make; to tell you that *it's all over now* between us, is something I couldn't do face to face.

It could not have been like, goodbye and *the shake of a hand.* I really am very sorry and if you were in my place, *you'd do the same for me* in trying to let you down without too much pain."

My *heartbroke* into a thousand pieces after reading the note and I headed to the *heartbreak side of town;* straight to the pub *down on the corner,* hoping that the *Genie in the bottle* would stop me wanting *someone else's dream.*

Three months after my *heartbroke,* I told myself that life can be *better than this* is now, so I decided to start picking up the pieces and to *move it on over* here to Australia for a while. *I'm doin' alright* now but I'll have to *hold on to my heart* a lot tighter now."

King looked back at Lady, who was laying in the sleeper compartment, then to Bo and said "I know how you feel, *been there done that* and you end up being *a better man* from the experience, but, there's *a little more to it than that.*

You look like a feller who believes and has faith in the creator, because he has *a bigger plan* for you and the pieces will fall into place, *one & one & one* at a time.

You have experienced *both side now* of love and heartbreak, but Cheryl, *she don't know it yet,* but she will soon discover *both sides* of love because she is in *someone else's dream* that is about to come true. He will *drive away* and *he'll have to go* to a place where the *Tequila sun rise* will not betray him for being a *two-steppin' fool.*

I believe in you and *love listens* to the prayers of people, and then it does what it can to make it happen. *I never go around mirrors* because I may miss something that I've never noticed before."

I looked at him strangely and said "You know you just said stuff that makes no sense to me. It's just like me saying to you that *I feel like Hank Williams tonight.* The big difference being; our skin colour is totally different."

King curiously asked "How far will you go for true love?"

I replied *"Forever is as far as I'll go,* if it's true love."

King nodded and said "Tenant Creek is just ahead and that's as far as I'm going. You will easily get another ride from the No *Doghouse* Food Roadhouse. Just mention that you had a ride with the *King of the road.*"

As I climbed down from the truck, King said to me *"Beauty's in the eye* of the person who can see inside another person.

20

Your *gypsy queen, Caroline,* is one of your *missing heroes* and has been, and always will be there for you. *That's what you call a friend.*

You can *call it love* on her part, but what about you and your part. *That's just how she gets* the *Tamworth blues* or the Kentucky blues. *I blame you* if you don't think on it, and *don't tell me* how you feel."

I jump out of the cabin saying "Thanks for the lift."

King replied "*You'd do the same for me* if I was on that stretch of road."

I was sad in a way to see the King drive off down the road, yet I was happy in another, because the conversations were getting a bit too weird for me.

In the roadhouse, it didn't take me long to find another ride going to Darwin, once I told the other truck drivers about my ride with the King and after they finished questioning me over it.

This next driver was a quiet, indigenous looking chap, and in the little conversation that we had, he asked me if *it raining at your home* and I told him that I didn't know 'cos I'm an overseas traveller, travelling through the outback.

When we reached Darwin, the driver let me out on the highway and told me that he was travelling on to Katherine and it would be better for me to stay in the big city.

He pointed and told me that *down on the corner* is *the house that Jack built,* next to his hotel, and that I'll get a room in there.

I booked into the Guest House for a week and then went to the hotel for a meal and a few drinks.

You know me, *when I'm drinking, the fighting side of me* can take over if I see someone in trouble, especially if it's a woman. Well, this woman asked me to dance with her, so I did.

While we were dancing, she said "*I can tell by the way you dance* that you've never done this style of dancing before."

She looked back at the group of people who she was with and quietly said "*I may never get to heaven,* but you seem an *easy* kinda guy to get along with so *would you lay with me* if I get a room."

I was shocked by her request and said "No. I don't think that that would be a very good idea. You go back to your friends and *I think I'll have another Bourbon* or two before I head off myself."

Then I heard coming from their table "Hey! *I want my rib back,* you can have the chips or salad and if *God made beer,* it would be better than this stuff you just bought me."

Another male replied "*I'll drink to that.*"

The female I was dancing with said "You drink that beer stuff, *way too fast.*"

A tall, stocky bloke stood up and pushed the female against the *walls* in the bar room and yelled "*I'd be worse off* if I drink that *Genie in the bottle* of whiskey like you do."

As he walked away, I went over to the female to see if she was alright and when the stocky male turned around and saw me with her, he pointed his finger at her and started yelling at her again "*Have I told you lately* that I think you're up to no good again, and, *I'm doin' alright* on my own. What you give me, *you call it love,* is not worth the trouble.

You and your *seven Spanish angels* had better get out of here before I do something that you'd be sorry for."

The next minute a fight broke out and many people left the hotel in a hurry but I copped one on the jaw. I'm *in the jailhouse now* and I don't know why."

Bo's writing was interrupted by the cell door opening.

"How you doing?" asked *Jackson.*

"*I'm doin' alright,* but can you tell me why I'm here?" I replied.

"You're in here for your own protection." said Jackson.

"The gentleman who threatened the Spanish girls came looking for you because he thought that you helped them get out of the hotel. He was ready to do you some serious injury or even kill you.

That particular gentleman and some of his friends have been charged with several crimes, two are so serious, that they are all in custody and being held in the maximum security section until they face court proceedings.

I suggest that you leave this town as soon as you can. How did you get here, by bus or plane?"

I replied "Neither. I was hitch hiking out from Mt Isa when the *King of the road* picked me up and took me as far as Tenant Creek where I got another lift to here."

Jackson's face went pale and he swallowed before saying "You were given a lift by the King of the road in Phantom 309.
Did he have an animal with him?"

"Yes." I said "A dog called Lady. Why?"

"Many years ago, a truck driver named David, gave his life to save the lives of seven females who had just arrived here from Spain. His truck was named Angel 309.

Every now and then, stories come in about sightings of this David and his truck. He has been nick named Earth Angel David because he is always helping someone in need when no other help is around. *Nobody knows* why he does it, he just does.

When you last saw him, what was he wearing and what did he look like?"

"Mmm, let me think. He had fair hair, unforgettable blue eyes and when he smiled, you couldn't really tell how old he was. He was wearing tight fitting blue jeans and a black fitted tee shirt.

He didn't seem to be like any other truck driver and I was aware that he was different, but I couldn't figure out in what way. I also remember him saying to me, "*Life don't have to mean nothin' at all*." and a lot of other weird stuff that I didn't understand. Plus, he knew of Caroline, my gypsy queen back home.

That particular piece of information never came up in conversation, so how did he know about her?"

Jackson said "Now; *that's what you call a friend* because of the fight and how it came about, *you gave me a mountain* of unsolvable clues to the crimes that you could have been charged with.

This David must have left so many tracks for me to follow, that it seems that we solved and made the arrests *way too fast* for it to be credible; but it is credible and it will stand up in court with the chance that the jail terms will be lengthy.

The females involved were also found and they are also in protective custody and will remain so until after the court cases and then they will be deported back to Spain because they over stayed their holiday visas.

I know that I shouldn't offer you this, but would you like a quick phone call to Caroline?"

"Yes please. If you could arrange that, I would love to speak with her, instead of sending her this letter." I said.

Jackson stayed in the room by the door while I spoke to Caroline and all he heard from my conversation was "*I'm doin' alright.* Yes, I am *a better man* than before. Yes, I think *it's still love. Have I told you lately* that I have *a bigger plan* for when I get home? *It's now or never. The older I get,* the more I want to ask you "*Will you be mine?*" I'll let you think on it and you can give me an answer when I get home. I have to go now and see if I can fly out of here later today or tomorrow."

I turned to Jackson and said "I think I will take the advice from that David person and go home to Caroline and thank you for all your time and help."

Jackson replied "No worries mate, *you'd done the same for me,* if we were in the opposite positions. Now go on get out of here before I get you charged with loitering."

REFERENCE

BEST SO FAR CD
BETTER THAN THIS
GYPSY QUEEN
HOUSE THAT JACK BUILT, THE
SHAKE OF A HAND, THE
CALL IT LOVE
GOD MADE BEER - (FEATURING THE BEER HOLDERS)
THAT'S WHAT YOU CALL A FRIEND
MISSING HEROES
I'M DOIN' ALRIGHT
GENIE IN THE BOTTLE
KING OF THE ROAD - (FEATURING JOHN WILLIAMSON)
STUCK IN THE MIDDLE - (FEATURING GUY SEBASTIAN)
EASY - (FEATURING WENDY MATTHEWS)
DRIVE AWAY - (FEATURING TANYA SELF)
GOOD ENOUGH FOR ME

BOTH SIDES NOW CD
STUCK IN THE MIDDLE - (FEATURING GUY SEBASTIAN)
EASY - (FEATURING WENDY MATTHEWS)
MOVE IT ON OVER - (FEATURING DAVID CAMPBELL)
BOTH SIDES - (FEATURING THE MCCLYMONTS)
DOWN ON THE CORNER - (FEATURING LEO SAYER)
KING OF THE ROAD - (FEATURING JOHN WILLIAMSON)
IT'S ALL OVER NOW - (FEATURING SHANNON NOLL)
SEVEN SPANISH ANGELS - (FEATURING TROY CASSAR-
DALEY)
IN THE JAILHOUSE NOW - (FEATURING KASEY CHAMBERS/
SHANE NICHOLSON)
HAVE I TOLD YOU LATELY - (FEATURING RENEE GEYER)
JACKSON - (FEATURING BECCY COLE)
MR BOJANGLES - (FEATURING TOMMY EMMANUEL)

CAN'T SETTLE FOR LESS CD
I'VE BEEN LOVED BY THE BEST
THAT'S JUST HOW SHE GETS
I WANT MY RIB BACK
THE BIGGEST FOOL
LADY LAY DOWN
GOD MADE BEER

THAT'S WHAT YOU CALL A FRIEND
CADILLAC TEARS
DOGHOUSE
MISSING HEROES
ONCE UPON A LONG TIME AGO
LIFE DON'T HAVE TO MEAN NOTHIN' AT ALL
ORPHAN OF THE ROAD

WORKIN OVERTIME CD
THE HOUSE THAT JACK BUILT
ONE & ONE & ONE
SHE'S GONE, GONE, GONE
WORKIN' OVERTIME (ON A GOOD TIME)
THE SHAKE OF A HAND
TWO-STEPPIN' FOOL
WHAT IT USED TO BE
BEAUTY'S IN THE EYE (OF THE BEERHOLDER)
BOATS TO BUILD
I'LL DRINK TO THAT
ONE OF A KIND
LITTLE BITTY THING CALLED LOVE
I FEEL LIKE HANK WILLIAMS TONIGHT

BOTH SIDES NOW: LTD EDTN TOUR PACK (W/PAL DVD) CD
STUCK IN THE MIDDLE FEATURING GUY SEBASTIAN
EASY FEATURING WENDY MATTHEWS
MOVE IT ON OVER FEATURING DAVID CAMPBELL
BOTH SIDES NOW FEATURING THE MCCLYMONTS
DOWN ON THE CORNER FEATURING LEO SAYER
KING OF THE ROAD
IT'S ALL OVER NOW FEATURING SHANNON NOLL
SEVEN SPANISH ANGELS FEATURING TROY CASSAR-DALEY
IN THE JAILHOUSE NOW FEATURING KASEY CHAMBERS
& SHANE NICHOLSON
HAVE I TOLD YOU LATELY FEATURING RENEE GEYER
JACKSON FEATURING BECCY COLE
MR BOJANGLES FEATURING TOMMY EMMANUEL

IM DOIN' ALRIGHT CD – IMPORT
I'M DOIN' ALRIGHT
SOMEONE ELSE'S DREAM
WAY TOO FAST
YOU'D DO THE SAME FOR ME

A BETTER MAN
FLOWERS
THE OLDER I GET
WALLS
HEARTBROKE
A BIGGER PLAN
GENIE IN THE BOTTLE
WILL YOU BE MINE
I'M DOIN' ALRIGHT (REPRISE)
SATURDAY NIGHT

SUGAR TALK CD – IMPORT
WHEN I'M DRINKING
GYPSY QUEEN
I BLAME YOU
HOLD ON TO MY HEART
GOODNIGHT SWEETHEART
TREAT ME LIKE A DOG
SUGAR TALK
I NEVER GO AROUND MIRRORS
I CAN TELL BY THE WAY YOU DANCE
CAROLINE
WHEN YOU LOVE SOMEBODY
LOVE LISTENS
IT'S STILL LOVE
DON'T TELL ME (YOU'RE NOT IN LOVE)

COWBOY DREAMS CD – IMPORT
LOVE BUG
CALL IT LOVE
WHEN LONELY MET LOVE
HUSH
SHE DON'T KNOW IT YET
COWBOY FOR A DAY
NOBODY KNOWS
LOUISIANA RENDEZVOUS
A LITTLE UNFAIR
A LITTLE MORE TO IT THAN THAT
ACTING A LITTLE CRAZY
LITTLE COWBOY DREAMS

THAT'S WHAT YOU CALL A FRIEND CD – IMPORT
THAT'S WHAT YOU CALL A FRIEND
LIFE DON'T HAVE TO MEAN NOTHING AT ALL
WOULD YOU LAY WITH ME (IN A FIELD OF STONE)

ADAM HARVEY / JOHN WILLIAMSON KING OF THE ROAD
CD SINGLE - IMPORT
KING OF THE ROAD

IM DOING ALRIGHT 2 CD
CD 1
I'M DOIN' ALRIGHT
SOMEONE ELSE'S DREAM
WAY TOO FAST
YOU'D DO THE SAME FOR ME
BETTER MAN
FLOWERS
THE OLDER I GET
WALLS
HEARTBROKE
A BIGGER PLAN
GENIE IN THE BOTTLE
WILL YOU BE MINE
I'M DOIN' ALRIGHT (REPRISE)
CD 2
A BIGGER PLAN
A BETTER MAN
WAY TOO FAST
YOU'D DO THE SAME FOR ME
FOREVER IS AS FAR AS I'LL GO
WHERE I COME FROM

SECOND TIME AROUND
HE LIVES MY DREAM
BEEN THERE DONE THAT
TEQUILA SUN RISE
I THINK I'LL HAVE ANOTHER BOURBON
THE FIGHTING SIDE OF ME
SAD SONGS AND WALTZES
BIG BAD JOHN
HELLO DARLIN'
TRASHY WOMEN
IT RAINING AT YOUR HOME

I'D BE WORSE OFF
I BELIEVE IN YOU

ADAM HARVEY – ADAM HARVEY
BAD LUCK WITH WOMEN
I MAY NEVER GET TO HEAVEN
IT'S NOW OR NEVER
SICK AND TIRED OF YOU
OLD DOGS AND CHILDREN AND WATERMELON WINE
YOU GAVE ME A MOUNTAIN
TAMWORTH BLUES
HE'LL HAVE TO GO
TIGHT FITTIN' JEANS
HEARTBREAK SIDE OF TOWN
PHANTOM 309
CHERYL MOANA MARIE

BIBLIOGRAPHY

Adam Harvey Picture: Courtesy Sony
Best So Far CD:
http://www.cduniverse.com/productinfo.asp?pid=8233704

Both Sides Now CD:
http://www.cduniverse.com/productinfo.asp?pid=8006920

Can't Settle For Less CD:
http://www.cduniverse.com/productinfo.asp?pid=7847365

Workin Overtime CD:
http://www.cduniverse.com/productinfo.asp?pid=7952819

Both Sides Now: LTD Edtn Tour Pack (W/Pal DVD) CD:
http://www.cduniverse.com/productinfo.asp?pid=8115828

Im Doin Alright CD – Import:
http://www.cduniverse.com/productinfo.asp?pid=7520619

Sugar Talk CD – Import:
http://www.cduniverse.com/productinfo.asp?pid=1425750

Cowboy Dreams CD – Import:
http://www.cduniverse.com/productinfo.asp?pid=5849742

That's What You Call A Friend CD – Import:
http://www.cduniverse.com/productinfo.asp?pid=6772152

Adam Harvey / John Williamson King Of The Road CD Single
– Import:
http://www.cduniverse.com/productinfo.asp?pid=8029714

Adam Harvey – Adam Harvey:
http://tjshouseofcountrymusic.blogspot.com/2010_06_01_archiv
e.html

Second Time Around:
http://tjshouseofcountrymusic.blogspot.com/2010_06_01_archiv
e.html

Im Doing Alright 2 CD:
http://tjshouseofcountrymusic.blogspot.com/2010_06_01_archiv
e.html

TROY CASSAR-DALEY

BIG CITY

Grandpa Damon was sitting out on his veranda, when his two grand-children, Ben and Hailey, came out and asked "Tell us a story, grandpa. Tell us a story please."

"What story do you want to hear? The one about *trains,* or *chasin' rodeo* clowns or the *big city* or when the *fisherman* caught the *yellow belly*." said grandpa.

"The *big city*." said Ben.

"No." said Haley "I want to hear about *chasin' rodeo* clowns."

"Now before you two start arguing, I'll tell you about both, starting with Ben's story." said grandpa.

"When I was young like you, I was a *real country* boy who used to *dream out loud* about saving up as much money as I could so that I could buy a *getaway car* and leave the *family farm*. Our farm was only *40 miles* down *River Road* from *River Town*.

Every weekend, my mum and I would drive to *River Town* to do some shopping and we would stay the night at my aunt's place.

I became friends with a *river boy* named Mick, who dreamt of becoming a deep sea *fisherman*.

He told me once, "Even though *I love this place,* and *River Town* will always be *my home town, someday* I'll be a *ramblin' man* and get *away from here*."

We always had, what we called, *good time Friday night* because we used to either sit around and listen to his big sister, Nat, play *her six stringer* guitar and *sing about this country* or we would *dream out loud*.

Sometimes our dreams were just made up fantasies, like I would say *I wish I was a train* so that I could go anywhere I want, or Mick would say he wished that he was a dolphin so that he could visit all the *islands in the stream* of the *big river country*.

He had a *big, big love* of being a *country boy fisherman,* lonesome but free up in the *River of Sorrow* territory.

I hated *going back home* to the *family farm* the next day after mum had finished all the shopping.

One evening, a few years later, while I was sitting in my room with the *bean pickin' blues,* I heard a little *bird on a wire chirping*. I went to the window and looked out to see this very beautiful but unusual looking blue *bird on a wire* that ran from the house to the shed.

I don't know why, but I told this bird about my *dream out loud* and then I heard in my head "*Everything's going to be alright*. Your *bitter tears* and *bean pickin' blues* will disappear once you're in your *getaway car* and driving away from here. When it's *time to say goodbye* to the *family farm,* it won't be a *sad goodbye* but, you will be *lonesome but free* and wear a *long black veil* over your heart for a while.

You will become a *factory man* and a *good woman's love* will be found amongst the *bar room roses* in a *V8 town Make the most of every day* and the *little things* that come your way but never *lay down to dance,* because the woman who waits *beyond the dancing,* well, she *ain't gonna change for you.*

You were *born to survive* with *no regrets* or *nightblindness. Time is a friend of mine* and will also be a friend to you. You *won't let the sun* disappear from your heart, but you will let it *rise and shine* for everyone. Go and *plant your fields* and get rid of your *bean pickin' blues* because *greater times* will come when you meet a *ramblin' man* who will *sing about this country.*"

The *bird on a wire* bobbed up and down twice, and then flew away into the night. I went back and sat on my bed wondering if I was starting to go crazy by hearing the voice in my head.

That weekend, the whole family went to *River Town,* so we could celebrate my eighteenth birthday. My friend Mick, the *river boy,* came and told me that it's *all over town,* that *Fred Brophy's in town* and this could be a way for us to get *away from here.*"

"Who?" I asked.

"*Fred Brophy's in town,* you know, the *factory man*. He travels the outback looking for a *country boy* or two to go work for him and *I wanna go back* with him.

You know who else is in town; Troy Cassar-Daley and he's down at the club. I've been rock and *rollin' with Troy Cassar-Dally* and my sister.

As she was playing her *six stringer* guitar, he began to *sing about this country*.

Nat was there setting up for tonight, when he walked in and heard her rehearsing her songs. He told her that she should move *away from here* and make a career for herself in music. I'll tell you now; I'm *losing my blues tonight* with Nat and Troy down at the club."

Mick and I went to the Coffee Lounge in the club and met with Fred Brophy who was interested in making me a *factory man,* but as for Mick; Fred just kept calling him a *river boy* until Mick got angry and told him "*I got a name* and it's Mick; not *river boy*."

Going back home with Mick after leaving the club, Mick said "I've been *down that road before* with people like him, they think that I should stay at the *dark end of the street* and cry my *bitter tears*. I can still *dream out loud* and once you've left, this *country boy* will be *walking away* from *my town* and heading for the *River of Sorrow* territory up in the *big river country*.

Even though *this town is me,* and *this day is mine,* I *ain't gonna change for you* or no-one else. I was *born to survive* and I ain't gonna stay in the *dark end of the street*. I may be *lonesome but free* now but *it's never too late* to get some *ladies in my life* and I will become a good *fisherman* and catch lots of *yellow belly*."

That blue *bird on a wire* said "That although my *buckets got a hole in it* right now, I should *make the most* of being a *river boy* now, because very soon I'll be a *wanted man* as the *yellow belly* will be travelling on *trains* all over this country. *The wind blows over* my heart and will continue to do so *till I gain control* of it." Yes, *I got a name* and everyone is gonna know it for the *yellow belly* and many more Australian fish products that I'll produce."

I looked at Mick and wondered if I should tell him that I too saw and heard the blue *bird on a wire* but my thoughts were distracted by the shouts of "*Fred Brophy's in town, Fred Brophy's in town* and he's looking for people to work in his factory."

A week later, I said my *sad goodbye* to my parents and told them "*I love this place* and *I love you both*. I won't miss the *bean pickin' blues*." and jumped into my old *getaway car* that I had finally bought and began my journey to become a *factory ma*n for the *Texas Swing* factory in Texas Queensland.

8 days after arriving in Texas, I was sitting in the *Old Texas Swing* Bowling Club and I spotted this beautiful young woman, sitting alone at a *table beyond the dancing* crowd. I watched her for a while before going over to her.

As I approached, I said to her "You look like you have the *bean pickin' blues,* so can I buy you a drink?"

She looked up at me and laughed before saying "That's a different pick up line and yes, I would like a drink, just coke thanks."

We sat and talked for a while and she told me her name was Maryanne. I found *the other side of lonely* that night in *sweet Maryanne,* and she was the best flower in the bunch of *bar room roses* in that club.

When we left the club, I offered to drive her home but she said that she would rather walk as she only lived down at the *end of the road,* so I offered to walk with her.

As we walked, we talked and she said *"When a small town dies,* everyone moves on, sadly *walking away* from their dreams. But everyone is *born to survive* the hard times if they can become strong enough. *I still can't say goodbye* to the memory and the shock on my family's faces when I told them I was leaving.

All dad could say was *"Why baby why?"* but I couldn't really explain the reason for my leaving; in fact, sometimes I can't even explain it to myself and why *walking away* from *my home town* was so important to me. *Going back home,* back to *my dreaming place* will never happen because the town isn't really there anymore.

You want to know something? *I still miss someone* that I hardly knew back home.

I was sitting in the small park in *my town* with *my old friend the blues,* when this *ramblin' man* came up and sat down beside me. Usually, I would get up and walk away but when he looked at me, I didn't feel scared, I just felt calm and warm inside. The *little things* I remember about him were his captivating blue eyes, his unusual smile, his beautiful hair and his ageless appearance.

We talked for a while, and then he said some things to me like *"Everything's going to be alright. Make the most of everyday* and continue being a *true believer.* Have *no regrets* about being *lonesome but free.* You were *born to survive* the path you're meant to travel.

You will meet an *original Australian working man* who has not had many ladies in his life. Going *beyond the dancing* will bring *big, big love* into your life, but don't wear the *long black veil* or sleep in *yesterday's bed* when you get to the *end of the road*. The *getaway car; ahh! They don't make 'em like that anymore. Time is a friend of mine* and he will be yours as well."

He got up and as he walked away he said "*Send me down your love* and as *long as I don't see you* with *bitter tears* or the *bean pickin' blues,* I'll be happy. *I'm an old man tryin' to live while I can.*"

My *biggest disappointment* was that I didn't know his name and I looked for him for a week after that meeting because I wanted answers to some things that he said that I didn't understand, but he must have moved on.

I listened as she spoke, but said nothing about my encounter with the bird. We agreed to meet the following evening for a meal at the *Texas Swing* Club and Maryanne was already there when I arrived.

During the meal, I heard some guy *sing about this country* and Maryanne looked over at him and said with a surprised voice "That guy singing is the man from the park who spoke to me." but before she could get over to talk to him, he had gone, and no one knew where he had gone to.

After she sat down again, I told her my encounter with the bird and also told her that my old friend Mick had had the same encounter with the bird. I also told her that the name of my old car was the *getaway car* and there haven't been many *ladies in my life.*

A *big, big love* developed between Maryanne and me and we moved to the *big city* for a few years. Of all the *ladies in my life,* my choice of the best flower in the bunch of *bar room roses* at the *Texas Swing* Bowling Club turned out to be your grandma.

Going back home to the *family farm* and *River Town* was something I had to do because my mother had become ill and I wanted to see my parents and family again.

Your grandma told me "You walked me to my *end of the road,* now *River Road; I want to walk that road with you.*"

As for Mick, the *river boy,* well, we bumped into him on *River Road* and he told us "When you left, I left and *I got a name* for myself as a fisherman. I'm not *lonesome but free* anymore but I do have three *ladies in my life,* my wife and twin daughters. I *make the most of everyday* with them.

Remember when we used to *dream out loud* and you said "*I wish I was a train*" so you could travel and I wished that I was a dolphin, so I could visit the islands; well in a way, both our dreams have come true.

I wonder what ever happened to that little unusual blue bird and I wonder if he has found a nest mate or if he's still flying around.

Maryanne said "I think he may still be *lonesome but free* and he will *make the most of everyday.*"

Their story was interrupted by their grandma who said, as she puts some afternoon tea down on the outside table, "I love this place and *I love you* all very much but sometimes *I still miss someone* that I met once in my old home town."

She looked and smiled at me because I knew that she meant the *ramblin' man;* the man who brought us together.

CHASIN' RODEO CLOWNS

"*I ain't gonna change for you.* I like *working in blues* and black because they don't show up the muck so much. *This day is mine* for working on the old horse float down in the shed. You know that *they don't make 'em like that anymore* so getting these parts wasn't easy or cheap. Now, we've been *down that road before* and unless I can get that horse float fixed, we'll never get *away from here.*

Usually *time is a friend of mine* but today I don't think it will be and just as *long as I don't see you* hanging around *Nightblindness,* that frisky colt, then I shouldn't have to put you in the *back blocks of home.*

Darn; *my buckets got a hole in it* and now I'll have to go next door and ask Dan for a loan of his. I don't have time to travel the *forty miles* to town to get another one." said Nobby to his cattle dog Tex.

Nobby called Tex into the Ute and together they drove over to Dan's place and pulling up near the shed where Dan was standing.

Dan said "You have to be *born to survive* running a mixed farm these days. The misses, *she wants* me to *plant your fields,* the ones that you don't use, with cabbages, but I told her that cabbages won't be any good down there 'cos they need to be attended to more often than say, wheat or cattle.

Sometimes *I wish I was a train* so I could get away from her and her whingin'. *Everything I do,* seems to get me into strife and I feel like moving out to the shed with *my old friend the blues.*"

"Don't knock a *good woman's love,* just remember, that she spends *everyday with you* and does all those *little things* around here that makes this house a home. She *ain't gonna change for you* and you won't change for her, not after all these years of being together. When was the last time you took her down to the Leagues Club for the evening?" said Nobby.

"I can't remember." said Dan. "Maybe I'll take her to the club at the end of the week. When I was in town the other day, people were talking *all over town* about a specialty act that was coming to the Leagues this weekend. People have been talking about some female whose able to play her *six stringer* guitar really well and they say that *she can sing about this country,* like an angel. Yep, I think I'll take the misses to the club for a *good time Friday night.*

Now, what did you come all the way over here for?" said Dan.

"*My buckets got a hole in it.* You know, the metal one that I bought recently, to drain the diff oil into. I need to fix the horse float in the next couple of days so Tex and I can start *chasin' rodeo* competitions from town to town." said Nobby.

"You're a bit old to start riding rodeo competitions again, aren't you and what about brumbies. Where will you get them from?" asked Dan.

"You're right, I am too old to start riding again and I couldn't anyway, not after that nasty accident that I had all those years back. I want to fix the float 'cos I have two brumbies that I wanna take to the rodeos for other riders to try and ride. An old mate from the *drovin' days* sent me down *Yer So Bad* and *Nightblindness. Yer So Bad* is the friskiest one and should give those lads a decent ride if I put them in the rider's draw.

Hey! *I'm an old old man tryin' to live while I can* and don't forget I'm *lonesome but free* to *make the most of everyday. I love this place* and *this town is me* but I think it's *time to say goodbye to my old friend the blues* and see if I can get some *ladies in my life again.*" said Nobby.

Dan thought for a few seconds as he looked around his shed and then he said "That nasty accident took the lot from you. It took *8 days* for you to come out of the coma to be then told that in your *last mile home,* you lost your career, lost your wife and almost lost your life.

You were *almost home* when that speeding crazy *wanted man* with a car full of *bar room roses* took your only *big, big love* away, leaving you *lonesome but free* and that *wanted man,* went *walking away* without a scratch. He also killed two of the females with him and injured another four; one of them seriously.

Ah! Here's the old bucket; you can keep it 'cos *they don't make 'em like that anymore* and here's a new one for a back up. I don't need them, as you can see, I have plenty of them." as he pointed to ten more buckets stacked upside down in a pyramid shape along the side wall of his shed.

Nobby looked over to the buckets and looked back to Dan before saying "*I wanna go back* to *my hometown; going back home* to *my dreaming place* where Martha is buried maybe the only way that I can say my *sad goodbye* to my only *big, big love. Chasin' rodeo* competitions maybe the *long way home,* but it's still *going back home.*

Along the way, *Yer So Bad* might make me a lot of money. You never know, someone might want to buy *Yer So Bad* and the other brumby. Now that would make me happy."

"You had better get going if you wanna fix that float and get *away from here*. My *biggest disappointment* is that I can't go with you like I used to and as *long as I don't see you* around *my town* for a while, then I'll know that you're alright. Take care now." said Dan.

"You take care of the misses and start giving her some *big, big love*."

Nobby laughed and continued saying "You'll be in the doghouse again 'cos she'll be wondering what you've been up to. Say "*I love you*." to her often and then you'll have her *under your spell again*."

Within two days, Nobby had fixed the horse float, loaded the brumbies in the float, Tex in the four wheel drive and was *40 miles* away from the first rodeo competition of the season.

He found a place to stay and tended to the animals before saying to Tex "You stay here and look after everything, I'm going to be *losin' my blues tonight,* something I haven't done in a long time."

The following day at the rodeo, Nobby didn't have much trouble in finding a *country boy* to ride his brumbies from the rider's draw. Someone even approached him and enquired as to where he got his float from because as the person said "*They don't make 'em like that anymore*."

He overheard one *country boy* say to an older man "That new brumby was a bit frisky and he easily threw me today. I wanna keep riding him if I can *till I gain control again* and stop him from throwing me. Find the owner and ask him if it's possible for me to keep riding him or if he is going to keep putting him in the rider's draw?"

A man and a young girl stopped behind him and he heard the girl say "Daddy, *I wish I was a train*."

The man replied "*Why baby why?*"

She came back with "*Trains* can go anywhere, so if I was one, I could go and visit grandma in heaven and give her these two prizes that I won."

The man and his daughter moved on and then he heard two females talking to each other on the other side of the rails where they had stopped.

The blonde female said "*This town is me* because it's a *V8 town* and *till I gain control again,* he's not going anywhere without me."

The dark haired female reply "*This day is mine. I won't let the sun go down* until I find a place and a way of *losin' my blues tonight.*"

Just as he was about to go and tend to his animals, a rodeo clown walked up to him and said "You have walked *down that road before* but this time *everything's going to be alright.* You will leave the *dark end of the street* when you go *beyond the dancing.* Your first *big, big love* does still *think about you* and says that if you *still can't say goodbye,* then don't. All *she wants* is for you to say to her "*Send me down your love.*" and she will, but in the form of another *big, big love.*

Keep *working in blues* but not black, for you will find that they will have you *going back home.* You are a *true believer* and were *born to survive;* to be able to live in *greater times. The wind blows over* our *one big land* and the sun will always *rise and shine* for you. *Someday* soon, you will find *the other side of lonely* and if you *dream out loud,* then your dreams will come true.

The *long black veil* you wore and the *bitter tears* you've shed because of the *wanted man* will have you picking up *yesterday's bed* and packing it away forever. Have *no regrets* because you will have the person from *beyond the dancing under your spell again.* Your first love says "*I love you* and I *ain't gonna change for you* and don't you change for no-one."

As the clown walked away and disappeared into the crowd, he looked back, smiled and said "You fixed the diff on the float really well and *they don't make 'em like that anymore.*"

Nobby stood there stunned and thought "Who was that guy and how did he know about my past and fixing my float? Actually, he didn't really look like a clown at all; he wasn't as rough and tough as you would expect a rodeo clown to be.

Really he had the same kind of blue eyes that my late wife had, soft and loving and his smile was not like any other males smile."

From that day on, Nobby started *chasin' rodeo* clowns, looking for the blue eyed clown to get some answers and explanations from him but he couldn't find him.

One day, while *working in blues* next to the slip rail, he met a very old school friend's sister, Marie, who he barely remembered.

41

Marie recognized him and went over and spoke to him first. They talked for about fifteen minutes and agreed to catch up that evening at the local hotel.

Over the meal they had ordered, Marie said "*When a small town dies,* many people start *walking away* from country living. My eldest brother Jerry left to drive *interstate* trains and became a *country boy lost in the city,* Mark stayed at home to help on the farm and I moved down here. *I love this place, this town is me* but sometimes *I wish I was a train* so that I could go to the places that my older brother goes.

I am a *true believer* in destiny. I was married to a much older man and when he passed away, I stayed in *my dreaming place* until I met the rodeo clown at the local showground. He told me that "*Till I gain control again* over my life, I will always find the *long way home* and *why baby why* do you want to go that way."

He told me that I've walked *down that road before,* but a *brighter day* is heading my way. Never again should *I wish I was a train* because *trains* only travel from one place to another and then back again, no variations or changes. Living my life like that would be boring and very uneventful.

He said that my late husband often does *think about you* and *won't let the sun go down* or stay down on you because you need it *to rise and shine* each day. I had to *make the most of everyday* and keep doing all those *little things, till I gain control again.* He told me that *you will believe in me* again and *this day is mine* to enjoy.

Someday another *true believer* will come along and he too has been *down that road before.* You'll know him because *you can't take the country out of the boy* where his brumbies and dog is concerned."

He disappeared into the crowd but I still remember those blue eyes and the smile that was just like my late husband's smile. I started *chasin' rodeo* clowns in every town that the rodeo went but I never saw him again and that was two years ago".

Nobby said "Did you say a rodeo clown with blue eyes, smiled and talked with you two years ago?"

"Yes. Why, have you seen him too?" asked Marie.

42

"Yes, I think so. He walked over and spoke to me and that was early one morning last week, I think. Do you think it's the same person?" said Nobby.

Marie stared at the bar and said "Is that him; the rodeo clown?"

Nobby turned and saw the clown raise his glass to them, smile, put his glass down on the bar and disappear through one of the doors in the back of the room.

"That's him!" exclaimed Nobby.

Marie said "It's a *long way home* for you. Is there anybody waiting for you there?"

Nobby said "No. *I'm an old man tryin' to live while I can. I wanna go back* to my farm and *my town* in the next few weeks because I think that it's time for me to sell up and move on. If you want to, you can come with me for a short holiday. I'll only be away for *eight days*."

"Why not." said Marie "*It's never too late* to start doing different things. I know that you *still can't say goodbye* completely to your past and *I still miss someone* but *I wanna go back* with you just as *long as I don't see you* become a negative person. I will never *wish I was a train* again because *this town is me, I love this place* and now, *this day is mine*."

Nobby laughed and said "*This day is mine* too. I really feel like *losing my blues tonight,* losing them for good and I think that it would be a *really good thing*. I think that I'll be able to sell my brumbies and then I may stick around here for a bit, that is, if you don't mind."

"*I can get used to that*." said Marie "When I *think about you* and the *little things* that you do and say, it makes me think that *everything I do* helps you to feel good."

Nobby raised his glass and looked into Marie's brown eyes and said "*People get ready* because Marie and I are coming and we *won't let the sun go down on this love. Time is a friend of mine,* so he'll give me as much time as I want to live the rest of my life."

Marie just looked at him and smiled as she raised her glass. She also whispered "Thank you rodeo clown. Whoever you are, you are now my angel."

"Grandpa." said Hailey "Have you ever met the rodeo clown?"

"No, I haven't, but your grandma believes he is an earth angel called David who goes around helping people when they need help."

Then grandpa said "I think that's enough stories for now, besides isn't that your grandma calling us in for some afternoon tea. You can go in and ask her about the rodeo clown."

REFERENCE

BRIGHTER DAY 2009
GOING BACK HOME
LONESOME BUT FREE
AWAY FROM HERE
TIME IS A FRIEND OF MINE
FISHERMAN
GETAWAY CAR
MY TOWN
WANTED MAN
LONG AS I DON'T SEE YOU
FAMILY FARM
WALKING AWAY
RIVER TOWN
YELLOW BELLY [INSTRUMENTAL]

I LOVE THIS PLACE
SING ABOUT THIS COUNTRY
CHASIN' RODEO
BIG, BIG LOVE
I LOVE THIS PLACE
DOWN THAT ROAD BEFORE
AIN'T GONNA CHANGE FOR YOU
THIS DAY IS MINE
COUNTRY BOY (LOST IN THE CITY)
BEAN PICKIN' BLUES
FRED BROPHY'S IN TOWN
I LOVE YOU
WON'T LET THE SUN (GO DOWN ON THIS LOVE)

BORN TO SURVIVE: THE BEST OF TROY CASSAR-DALEY
BORN TO SURVIVE
LONESOME BUT FREE
THEY DON'T MAKE 'EM LIKE THAT ANYMORE
EVERYTHING'S GOING TO BE ALRIGHT
TRUE BELIEVER
GOING BACK HOME
I WISH I WAS A TRAIN
BIRD ON A WIRE
BIGGEST DISAPPOINTMENT
LITTLE THINGS
RIVER BOY
LAST MILE HOME

BAR ROOM ROSES
LADIES IN MY LIFE
MAKE THE MOST (OF EVERYDAY WITH YOU)
DREAM OUT LOUD
RAMBLIN' MAN
I WANNA GO BACK
TRAINS
WALKING AWAY
ROLLIN' WITH TROY CASSAR-DALEY [DVD][*]
BIRD ON A WIRE [DVD][*]
ISLANDS IN THE STREAM [DVD][*]

LONG WAY HOME/BORROWED AND BLUE
RIVER ROAD
RISE AND SHINE
BORN TO SURVIVE
THINK ABOUT YOU
40 MILES
LONG WAY HOME
MY DREAMING PLACE
WISH I WAS A TRAIN
NIGHTBLINDNESS
SAD GOODBYE
MAKE THE MOST (OF EVERYDAY WITH YOU)
8 DAYS (FROM SYDNEY)
EVERYTHING I DO
FACTORY MAN
MY OLD FRIEND BLUES
RIVER BOY
YER SO BAD
BIG CITY
DARK END OF THE STREET
WHY BABY WHY
I GOT A NAME
TILL I GAIN CONTROL AGAIN
LOSIN' MY BLUES TONIGHT
I STILL MISS SOMEONE
MY BUCKETS GOT A HOLE IN IT
I'M AN OLD MAN TRYIN' TO LIVE WHILE I CAN
STILL CAN'T SAY GOODBYE
[UNTITLED HIDDEN TRACK]

BRIGHTER DAY 2005
GOING BACK HOME
LONESOME BUT FREE
AWAY FROM HERE
TIME IS A FRIEND OF MINE
FISHERMAN
GETAWAY CAR
MY TOWN
WANTED MAN
LONG AS I DON'T SEE YOU
FAMILY FARM
WALKING AWAY
RIVER TOWN
YELLOW BELLY
BIRD ON A WIRE
SOMEDAY
LONG BLACK VEIL
TILL I GAIN CONTROL AGAIN - LIVE
MAKE THE MOST (OF EVERY DAY WITH YOU) - LIVE

I WISH I WAS A TRAIN 2003
I WISH I WAS A TRAIN
SOMEDAY
LONG BLACK VEIL

BORROWED & BLUE 2004
FACTORY MAN
MY OLD FRIEND THE BLUES
RIVER BOY
YER SO BAD
BIG CITY
DARK END OF THE STREET
WHY BABY WHY
I GOT A NAME
TILL I GAIN CONTROL AGAIN
LOSIN' MY BLUES TONIGHT
I STILL MISS SOMEONE
MY BUCKETS GOT A HOLE IN IT
I'M AN OLD OLD MAN TRYIN' TO LIVE WHILE I CAN
STILL CAN'T SAY GOODBYE

LONG WAY HOME 2002
RIVER ROAD
RISE AND SHINE

BORN TO SURVIVE
THINK ABOUT YOU
40 MILES
LONG WAY HOME
MY DREAMING PLACE
WISH I WAS A TRAIN
NIGHTBLINDNESS
SAD GOODBYE
MAKE THE MOST (OF EVERYDAY WITH YOU)
8 DAYS (FROM SYDNEY)
EVERYTHING I DO

BEYOND THE DANCING 1994
MY HOME TOWN
DREAM OUT LOUD
END OF THE ROAD
WORKING IN BLUES
BEYOND THE DANCING
PLANT YOUR FIELDS
TEXAS SWING
BITTER TEARS
SIX STRINGER
SEND ME DOWN YOUR LOVE
GREATER TIMES
NO REGRETS
BEYOND THE DANCING (REPRISE)
RAMBLIN' MAN
OLD TEXAS SWING
BITTER TEARS
RIVER OF SORROW

BIG RIVER
THEY DON'T MAKE 'EM LIKE THAT ANYMORE
BIG RIVER COUNTRY
I WANNA GO BACK
ALL OVER TOWN
THE OTHER SIDE OF LONELY
TRAINS
IT'S NEVER TOO LATE
TIME TO SAY GOODBYE
UNDER YOUR SPELL AGAIN
I WANT TO WALK THAT ROAD WITH YOU
V8 TOWN
ONE BIG LAND

48

WHEN A SMALL TOWN DIES
THE DROVING DAYS

TRUE BELIEVER
GOOD WOMAN'S LOVE
SHE WANTS
LITTLE THINGS
I CAN GET USED TO THAT
TRUE BELIEVER
LADIES IN MY LIFE
SWEET MARYANNE
YOU WILL BELIEVE IN ME
THE WIND BLOWS OVER (THE LONELY OF HEART)
LAY DOWN AND DANCE
BAR ROOM ROSES
GOOD TIME FRIDAY NIGHT
BACK BLOCKS OF HOME

BORN TO SURVIVE THE DVD
BORN TO SURVIVE
THEY DON'T MAKE 'EM LIKE THAT ANYMORE
I WISH I WAS A TRAIN (WITH PAUL KELLEY)
END OF THE ROAD
LITTLE THINGS
GOING BACK HOME
RAMBLIN' MAN (WITH TOMMY EMMANUEL)
I WANNA GO BACK
FACTORY MAN
DREAM OUT LOUD
GETAWAY CAR (WITH KASEY CHAMBERS)
TRAINS
LADIES IN MY LIFE
RIVER BOY (WITH SHANE HOWARD)
TRUE BELIEVER
YER SO BAD
LONESOME BUT FREE
EVERYTHING'S GOING TO BE ALRIGHT

TROY CASSAR-DALEY LIVE CD
SING ABOUT THIS COUNTRY
THEY DON'T MAKE 'EM LIKE THAT ANYMORE
RIVER TOWN
BAR ROOM ROSES
LONESOME BUT FREE

I LOVE THIS PLACE
CHASIN' RODEO
MAKE THE MOST (OF EVERYDAY WITH YOU)
BRIGHTER DAY
RIVER BOY
I WISH I WAS A TRAIN
BIRD ON A WIRE (FEAT. JIMMY BARNES)
BORN TO SURVIVE
EVERYTHING'S GOING TO BE ALRIGHT
YESTERDAY'S BED
BEAN PICKIN' BLUES
BIGGEST DISAPPOINTMENT (FEAT. JOY MCKEAN)
THIS TOWN IS ME
LOSIN' MY BLUES TONIGHT
LITTLE THINGS
TRAINS
PEOPLE GET READY
COUNTRY BOY (LOST IN THE CITY)
THIS DAY IS MINE
DREAM OUT LOUD
BIG, BIG LOVE

ALMOST HOME
DISC 1
ALMOST HOME
BIG RIVER COUNTRY
TRUE BELIEVER
I WANNA GO BACK
BITTER TEARS
YOU CAN'T TAKE THE COUNTRY OUT OF THE BOY
THE OTHER SIDE OF LONELY
DREAM OUT LOUD
WORKING IN BLUES
V8 TOWN
SIX STRINGER
BAR ROOM ROSES
THE WIND BLOWS OVER (THE LONELY OF HEART)
NO REGRETS
RAMBLIN' MAN
TEXAS SWING
DISC 2
ALL OVER TOWN
BEYOND THE DANCING
MY HOMETOWN

IT'S NEVER TOO LATE
GOOD WOMAN'S LOVE
UNDER YOUR SPELL AGAIN
WHEN A SMALL TOWN DIES
LADIES IN MY LIFE
TRAINS
THE RIVER OF SORROW
SHE WANTS
LITTLE THINGS
GOOD TIME FRIDAY NIGHT
THEY DON'T MAKE 'EM LIKE THAT ANYMORE
ORIGINAL AUSTRALIAN WORKING MAN
TIME TO SAY GOODBYE

I LOVE THIS PLACE LIMITED EDITION CD/DVD
CD
SING ABOUT THIS COUNTRY
CHASIN' RODEO
BIG, BIG LOVE
I LOVE THIS PLACE
DOWN THAT ROAD BEFORE
AIN'T GONNA CHANGE FOR YOU
THIS DAY IS MINE
THIS TOWN IS ME
COUNTRY BOY (LOST IN THE CITY)
BEAN PICKIN' BLUES
FRED BROPHY'S IN TOWN
I LOVE YOU
WON'T LET THE SUN (GO DOWN ON THIS LOVE
DVD
BIG BIG LOVE
AIN'T GONNA CHANGE FOR YOU
THIS TOWN IS ME
COUNTRY BOY (LOST IN THE CITY)
BEAN PICKIN' BLUES

I LOVE THIS PLACE VINYL
SIDE ONE
1 SING ABOUT THIS COUNTRY
2 CHASIN' RODEO
3 BIG, BIG LOVE
4 I LOVE THIS PLACE
5 DOWN THAT ROAD BEFORE
6 AIN'T GONNA CHANGE FOR YOU

7 THIS DAY IS MINE
SIDE TWO
1 THIS TOWN IS ME
2 COUNTRY BOY (LOST IN THE CITY)
3 REALLY GOOD THING
4 BEAN PICKIN' BLUES
5 FRED BROPHY'S IN TOWN
6 I LOVE YOU
7 WON'T LET THE SUN (GO DOWN ON THIS LOVE)

I LOVE THIS PLACE STANDARD EDITION CD
SING ABOUT THIS COUNTRY
CHASIN' RODEO
BIG, BIG LOVE
I LOVE THIS PLACE
DOWN THAT ROAD BEFORE
AIN'T GONNA CHANGE FOR YOU
THIS DAY IS MINE
THIS TOWN IS ME
COUNTRY BOY (LOST IN THE CITY)
BEAN PICKIN' BLUES
FRED BROPHY'S IN TOWN
I LOVE YOU
WON'T LET THE SUN (GO DOWN ON THIS LOVE)

WANTED MAN CD
DISC 1
BORROWED AND BLUE
FACTORY MAN
MY OLD FRIEND THE BLUES
RIVER BOY
YER SO BAD
BIG CITY
DARK END OF THE STREET
WHY BABY WHY
I GOT A NAME
TILL I GAIN CONTROL
LOSIN' MY BLUES TONIGHT
I STILL MISS SOMEONE
MY BUCKETS GOT A HOLE IN IT
I'M AN OLD MAN TRYIN' TO LIVE WHILE I CAN
STILL CAN'T SAY GOODBYE
DISC 2
BRIGHTER DAY

GOING BACK HOME
LONESOME BUT FREE
AWAY FROM HERE
TIME IS A FRIEND OF MINE
FISHERMAN
GETAWAY CAR
MY TOWN
WANTED MAN
LONG AS I DON'T SEE YOU
FAMILY FARM
WALKING AWAY
RIVER TOWN
YELLOW BELLY (INSTRUMENTAL)
DISC 3
LONG WAY HOME
RIVER ROAD
RISE AND SHINE
BORN TO SURVIVE
THINK ABOUT YOU
FORTY MILES
LONG WAY HOME
MY DREAMING PLACE
WISH I WAS A TRAIN
NIGHT BLINDNESS
SAD GOODBYE
EVERYDAY WITH YOU
EIGHT DAYS

BEYOND THE DANCING CD
MY HOME TOWN
DREAM OUT LOUD
END OF THE ROAD
WORKING IN BLUES
BEYOND THE DANCING
PLANT YOUR FIELDS
TEXAS SWING
BITTER TEARS
SIX STRINGER
SEND ME DOWN YOUR LOVE
GREATER TIMES
NO REGRETS
BEYOND THE DANCING (REPRISE)

BRIGHTER DAY - LIMITED CD
DISC 1
GOING BACK HOME
LONESOME BUT FREE
AWAY FROM HERE
TIME IS A FRIEND OF MINE
FISHERMAN
GETAWAY CAR
MY TOWN
WANTED MAN
LONG AS I DON'T SEE YOU
FAMILY FARM
WALKING AWAY
RIVER TOWN
YELLOW BELLY (INSTRUMENTAL)
DISC 2
BIRD ON A WIRE (WITH JIMMY BARNES)
SOMEDAY
LONG BLACK VEIL
TILL I GAIN CONTROL AGAIN (LIVE)
MAKE THE MOST (OF EVERY AWAY DAY WITH YOU) (LIVE)

TROY CASSAR-DALEY - TROY CASSAR-DALEY (2010)
THIS DAY IS MINE
CHASIN' RODEO
LONESOME BUT FREE
BIG BIG LOVE
I LOVE THIS PLACE
DOWN THAT ROAD BEFORE
LADIES IN MY LIFE
COUNTRY BOY (LOST IN THE CITY)
YESTERDAY'S BED
MAKE THE MOST (OF EVERYDAY WITH YOU)
GOING BACK HOME
AWAY FROM HERE

BIBLIOGRAPHY

Troy Cassar-Daley picture: Courtesy Roxanne Brown

Brighter Day2009: http://new.music.yahoo.com/troy-cassar-daley/albums/brighter-day--218822415

I Love This Place: http://new.music.yahoo.com/troy-cassar-daley/albums/i-love-this-place--218799185

Born to Survive: The Best of Troy Cassar-Daley: http://new.music.yahoo.com/troy-cassar-daley/albums/born-to-survive-the-best-of-troy-cassar-daley--200069853

Long Way Home/Borrowed and Blue: http://new.music.yahoo.com/troy-cassar-daley/albums/long-way-home-borrowed-and-blue--184745965

Brighter Day 2005: http://new.music.yahoo.com/troy-cassar-daley/albums/brighter-day--26213656

I Wish I Was a Train 2003: http://new.music.yahoo.com/troy-cassar-daley/albums/i-wish-i-was-a-train--191644710

Borrowed & Blue 2004: http://new.music.yahoo.com/troy-cassar-daley/albums/borrowed-blue--3812027

Long Way Home 2002: http://new.music.yahoo.com/troy-cassar-daley/albums/long-way-home--27756732

Beyond The Dancing 1994: http://new.music.yahoo.com/troy-cassar-daley/albums/beyond-the-dancing--144214

Big River: http://www.gumtreemusic.com.au/music/troy--cassar-daley/big-river.aspx

True Believer: http://www.gumtreemusic.com.au/music/troy--cassar-daley/true-believer.aspx

Born To Survive The DVD:
http://www.gumtreemusic.com.au/music/troy--cassar-daley/born-to-survivethe-dvd.aspx

Troy Cassar-Daley Live CD:
http://liberation.com.au/artists/release/Live_(Troy_Cassar-Daley_CD)

Almost Home: http://www.gumtreemusic.com.au/music/troy--cassar-daley/almost-home.aspx

I Love This Place Limited Edition CD/DVD:
http://www.gumtreemusic.com.au/music/troy--cassar-daley/i-love-this-place-ltd.aspx

I Love This Place Vinyl:
http://liberation.com.au/artists/release/I_Love_This_Place_(Vinyl)

I Love This Place Standard Edition CD:
http://www.gumtreemusic.com.au/music/troy--cassar-daley/i-love-this-place-standard-edition.aspx

Wanted Man CD: http://www.gumtreemusic.com.au/music/troy--cassar-daley/wanted-man.aspx

Beyond The Dancing CD:
http://www.gumtreemusic.com.au/music/troy--cassar-daley/beyond-the-dancing.aspx

Brighter Day - Limited CD:
http://www.gumtreemusic.com.au/music/troy--cassar-daley/brighter-day-limited.aspx

Troy Cassar-Daley - Troy Cassar-Daley (2010):
http://www.certifiedguitarplayer.com/troycassar-daley-troycassar-daley2010.aspx

JAMES BLUNDELL

CONVERSATIONS

Paul, Simon, Dave, John and Rick all received a letter that read "*Let's all get together* at *the Poet And The Queen* Hotel for the next Tamworth Country Music Festival. Accommodation has been booked and paid for. It's been a long time since we all worked together *down on the farm.*

I thought that seeing it's only the beginning of November that would give you enough time to arrange your affairs and travel to Tamworth.

It's a *beautiful day in New York* and I fly out of here tomorrow. I hope that you can all make it so we can take a short walk down *Memory Lane.*"

The letter was unsigned and the post mark was unreadable so that made it intriguing for each recipient of the letter.

*   *   *   *   *

The end of January soon came and the five men had checked into the hotel. Three of them met in the bar and the conversations started:

Paul: "I was working *way out west* when I got the letter that was sent and the only way I could get here was on the *Greyhound buses* that took two days of tiring and boring travelling. I think it wouldn't have been so bad if the countryside wasn't all the same, even the townships looked the same after the third town we stopped at for a meal."

Simon: "I had a bit of travelling to do myself from up in the *Greylands*. I swear that that place is *higher than heaven*. I had to get a lift to the nearest station to catch the *fast train* down to Sydney and then another train to get here. How did you get here, *young John Taylor?"*

John: "Hey, cut that out, it's just John now. I'm working in *Texas, Qld.* Yeah, I heard *Queensland calling* and I answered it. Candy, my *blue heeler, my old friend and General Lee,* my ute, travelled all the way down on the New England Highway".

Simon: "I wonder if the other two are coming. You know that Rick became a professional boxer and travelled a fair bit overseas. I got *postcards from Saigon,* when he was over there and at one time I got a snap shot of him eating this *Amsterdam breakfast* in the courtyard of this posh looking restaurant."

Paul: "Amsterdam is somewhere up Holland way, isn't it? I don't think that I could go up there, it's too cold for me and I'm *bound to freeze* my arse off not to mention other parts of my body. I certainly would need someone to keep me warm."

Rick: "*I don't fight anymore.* Paul, I doubt that they'll let you into the country. You have to be over *four feet tall* unless you're a kid to get in and the only thing that you'll get to keep you warm is a blanket and that's if you're lucky."

Paul looked around as the other guys laughed and Rick and Dave sat down and ordered a couple of drinks.

Rick: "You still drinking your usual?"

Dave nodded his head, yes.

Rick: "Barman; a beer and a coke. You know that *the old man's gone.* They say that he had too much *time on his hands.* He went for a ride down to *the valley,* but his horse made it back alone to the stable. They found the *old man* under the shade of some rocks and bushes after a long search. No-one can figure out exactly what might have happened because he was such a good horseman."

Simon: "How did his family take it?"

Rick: "You know how his wife was with religion and faith. She was naturally upset but after the funeral, she seemed to accept his passing and tried to carry on with the farm. Oh, I'm not knocking it but some people don't believe in that stuff."

Dave: "We don't live in the *dark ages* anymore. People have started to believe in *Guardian Angels* and the *Age of Grace.* Some say that their God works in *mysterious ways* therefore, they aren't afraid to admit that he exists."

John: "This talk is getting a bit heavy for me at the moment. I say that if you believe in it yourself, you shouldn't go pushing your beliefs on anyone else unless they ask you to. So *Mr Richie,* what have you been up to since you left the farm?"

Rick: "Now that *the old man's* gone, I'm the manager *down on the farm.* Mrs. T couldn't handle it all by herself so she asked me to help since I had been with them since I was a lad and knew what had to be done to keep the place going. That's *all that I need* to do, seeing that *I'm older now.*"

Simon: "Dave, what have you been up to? Are you still a *lunatic for love* and hanging around the *doctor's daughter* or did she see sense and give you the flick?"

Dave: "Nah, that finished years ago, you *can't love alone.* She wasn't
a *perpetual child. Her sweet love* was like a *ring around the
moon,* kept coming and going and she finally went. She just
took off one day and that was it. *Love don't speak to me*
anymore."

Paul: "I can't believe that *the old man's gone.* He was *nature's
gentleman.* He was a *brilliant man* who would do a *handshake
deal* and stick to it. There aren't many people around these
days that would do as he did. Everyone wants you to put stuff
in writing before they will even talk to you."

Rick: "*Nature's gentleman,* a *portrait of a man* that no-one can be
compared to. People used to say that *there walks a man* with
pride and respect for everyone he meets, no matter who they
are."

The music that was playing from a jukebox in the corner of the bar was
the *Cloncurry Cattle song* and as John got up to go over to put more
music on, he spotted his *blue heeler* dog, Candy, standing in an open
doorway.

John: "Candy, you're a *bad girl;* you know that you're not allowed in
here. I left you with plenty of *water* in the shade. All right, I
know that look *in your eyes;* let's go outside and I'll give you a
touch of water from the hose I saw by the rainwater tank to cool
you down."

John walked out back taking Candy with him, Paul went to the bar and
ordered more drinks and Dave went over to the jukebox and stood there
for a while before he selected a couple more songs to play.

Simon: "Dave, he hasn't really changed except he's a quiet bloke now,
he doesn't seem to be as out going as he used to be. I can't
believe that a bloke with those blue eyes and nice smile *ain't
got love* in his life."

Rick: "He had the *perfect world* but it came crashing down on him.
He had a girl named *Libby* when he was living and working in
the Kimberleys for a while. They were on a *dream ride* under
the *Kimberley moon,* when he asked her to marry him. He let
love get in the way of common sense, 'cos they hadn't known
each other for very long.

One day, not long after he had asked her, a troupe of *dancers* went to the town where they were living and when they left, Libby went with them, *running down the sun* before it disappeared on the other side of *the Great Divide*. The *Kimberley moon* disappeared in the *deluge* of heartbreak and tears. Yes, tears; he's really a sensitive bloke you know. You can say *forgive and forget,* but I don't know if he has 'cos his *hurt is on the inside."*

Dave came back and sat down just as his first selected song started to play, Paul put the round of drinks down on the table that they had moved to and John returned carrying *postcards from Saigon* in his left hand.

John: "Rick did you ever *fight naked* like one of those other boxers did. I can't remember his name right now? I found these postcards in a box a couple of days before I left Texas. On this one you mention *Bandy, Dylan Diana & God* but you never said who they were."

Rick: "Bandy, Dylan, Diana were three kids who were living in *this poor town* and the way they made their money to buy food was to sing a *song for a hero,* and their hero was God. They believed in him and that he would help them to survive. It was *a very good song* but most of the tourists would just *walk on* by without even noticing them. Pretty sad really."

Paul: "Anyone got the time?"

Dave: *"Two to one.* Why?"

Paul: "I'm getting hungry, how 'bout lunch?"

Dave: "I'll be in that. What about you guys?"

The boys all nodded yes and picked up their drinks and walked into the Dining room.

Dave   *"Honey hey;* are we still in time to get some lunch?"

The waitress walked over to their table and took their orders and returned about fifteen minutes later with one mixed grill, one burger with chips, two steak, egg and chips and one, fish and chips. When the guys had finished eating, they went to pay for the meals and were told that all meals eaten in the hotel, and all your drinks were already paid for.

61

Dave looked up at the waitress and smiled. She bent down and whispered something in his ear and he just nodded yes. She whispered something else that made Dave chuckle before she walked away towards the kitchen.

Simon: "Better watch it mate, she'll get a *touch in love* with you and really all she'll really want is a *24 hour love affair* that will bring you nothing but trouble in the end. You'd be better off getting a dog. *She won't let you down* and she'll love you forever.

I have a question to ask all of you? Which one of you guys is picking up the tab for this get together?"

John: "Candy loves me no matter what. I actually found her when she was a pup, walking down *this road* on the outskirts of Uralla I stopped and picked her up and I looked around to see if I could find her mother or a family who she might have wandered away from, but she was on her own. Someone might have just stopped and abandoned her. She was a pretty little thing and I told her that I like *the sound of your smile*. I stopped in Uralla to see if anyone was missing the pup, but nobody knew anything about her so I took her with me and we've been together ever since.

Yeah, which one of you is rich enough to pay for all this? I know that it's not me, that's for sure."

Rick: "Don't look at me. I made a bit of money from fighting but it wasn't enough to pay for this shindig. Simon, what's it like where you live?"

Simon: "Everyone is *drowning in this drought* up in the *Greylands*. We pray just to hear *rain on a tin roof* and when we do get some rain, it's never enough to really do anything but give you *cabin fever* due to the humidity. There is a mixture of employment up there; mining, cattle stations and farms that produce a number of different crop all year round.

As for me paying for this shindig, you must be joking; anyway I wouldn't have known how to find you all. I live in the sticks remember and to even try to find someone else to find you would be near impossible."

Dave: "In the Kimberleys, when we heard *rain on a tin roof,* we used to race outside to catch the rain *water* in buckets or any other type of container that was at hand. Nearly every place had rain water tanks but most times there wasn't enough rain to put into the tanks. Yeah, so I lived in a place near the tropics but that doesn't mean that we got rain like the other places do. The only time that we got some decent rain was one year when a cyclone went through and we were lucky to get some of it."

Paul: "*Way out west,* water is *something sacred.* You can drive for miles down *this road* and all you'll see in the rear vision mirror is *dust.* Even in *the valley,* there is *the tree* that, by now, should be eight foot high but it's only *four feet tall* because of the lack of water. A lot more rain is needed to ease the water crisis that is happening out there. I know of a farmer who has had to drill another bore to get the water he needs for his live-stock."

Dave: "Yes, we need the rain, but we need it to come down in *moderation* and not continuously heavy because that washes away the top soil and leaves us with more problems. Many people who live on the coast and even on the fringe of the outback country don't really know what it's like not to have rain for months on end and when it does rain, the ground is so dry that it soaks in and then dries out quickly."

Paul: "Maybe if *nature's gentleman* could talk to the *Guardian Angels* of this land and tell them that this is the *Age of Grace,* they might be able to give us a bit more rain more often. We need enough to kill this drought and set our land back on track."

Rick: "A farmer never has enough *time on his hands,* as you guys know and the *Age of Grace* or God's *mysterious ways* will never stop people from *walking away* from the land when they've had enough. *Down on the farm,* it's *all up to me* to it keep running smoothly and as long as I can *be strong* and keep my *pride* in myself and my working abilities, then I'll make sure *nothing's going to get me down.*"

John: "Hey, anybody got the time?"

Dave: "The clock above the bar says *five to five*".

John: "I don't know about you other guys, but I think I'll go and have a bit of a play with Candy, feed her and then go clean up a bit and get back down here before the evening meal rush starts. I figure that with the festival in town, there's going to be a heck of a lot more people in here every night for food and to listen to whatever band or artist that's gonna be playing."

Paul: "I think you may be right there so let's meet back here around six thirty, which should give us enough time to do what we want to do."

They all got up and John took off out the back to attend to Candy, Paul headed over to the bar for another drink, Simon and Rick headed up stairs to their rooms.

Dave headed out back to where John was laying out a bed roll for Candy.

Dave: "John, this is the *Age of Grace*. You will find it in Candy's new pup and you will call it Grace. Keep your *postcards from Saigon* as they will bring you happiness. The empty feeling that you have inside will disappear soon and when it does, you will find yourself *moving on* with a special someone from the postcard."

John stood up from setting out Candy's bed roll and turned around to see Dave walking back into the hotel.

John: "Whatever Dave said, didn't make much sense. Candy, I know that you can't have pups; or can you? We've tried to mate you many times but without success. When we get back home, I'll have to take you out in the paddocks to chase some sheep around.
You've had it too easy lately. I'll catch up with Dave later and ask him to explain what he meant."

Dave found Paul still at the bar drinking and filling out a Keno coupon.

Dave "Paul, that coupon will give you a decent win. As you travel back *across the miles, the 7:45* bus will be *way out west* when you will have to *slow it down* near the Range Road *signpost*. You will be *so close to home* when the *load* on a truck in front of your bus shifts, causing the truck to roll. You are never *too old to die young* and neither you nor anyone else will die and there will be no damage to the bus either. You will know the exact *moment in time* to act and it will be when you hear the *Cloncurry Cattle song*. The driver will listen to you and do as you say without question."

Paul put his pen and drink down to turn and ask Dave what he was on about, but as he turned, he saw Dave's back heading out the door towards the stairs to the upstairs rooms.

Paul thought: "I'll catch up with him in half an hour and ask him what he was on about when we have our meal. Those numbers on the Keno screen from the last game are all mine. I've won something decent like Dave said I would. How did he know that I was going to win?"

Dave went upstairs and knocked on Simon's door and was invited in. Simon was sitting on his bed doing something with his shoes that he was putting on and didn't pay much attention to Dave standing there.

Dave: "Simon, Where you live is *higher than heaven* and there you will sing a *song for Louise* under the *Kimberley moon*. You will hear the *rain on a tin roof* and see the *rainbows* from the *postcards from Saigon*. There will be a man from a good business, with *time on his hands* and he will *hand it down* to you. *I'm afraid* that *hard times* will be with you for another couple of years but *learning to roll* with the times will help you.
This is the truth when I say that God does work in *mysterious ways* and there are *Guardian Angels* out there so have faith and don't be *weary of this world*. It has been *so good to meet you* and to answer this question that you often fear "*Who do you trust;* yourself, God or other people who have different opinions and different answers?" Put some faith in God if you believe in him but most of all; trust and have faith in yourself to do the right thing. Don't ever become *a fool such as I.*"

Dave turned and walked out the door towards Rick's room. Simon put on his shoe and chased after him, catching a glimpse of him disappearing into Rick's room. Simon went over and knocked on Rick's door, but no answer came from inside the room. *Meanwhile*, both John and Paul had come up to the rooms looking for Dave.

Simon: "I think Dave just went into Rick's room but when I knocked a minute ago, I got no answer from anyone. Did Dave or Rick pass you on the way up?"

John: "We came up together and no-one passed us going either way. Is there *any other way out?*"

Simon: "I don't think so. Let's go in and see if Rick's ok."

65

Paul: "Yeah, maybe Dave's saying some weird stuff to Rick now. Has Dave said any weird stuff to you guys at all today?"

Both John and Simon acknowledge Paul with a nod of their heads as they opened the door to Rick's room. They were surprised to find the room completely empty and looking like no-one had ever been in there. They closed the door and headed for Dave's room, only to find it exactly as they had found Rick's room, completely empty.

Paul: "What do you make of that? We all saw and talked to them, but their rooms are empty."

Simon: "Maybe when they got here, they didn't bring up their gear so they're down getting it now. I'm going down for a drink and catch up with them when they come to eat. You guys coming with me or are you just gonna stay here?"

Paul: "I'm coming; I really do need a drink now."

John: Yeah, I'm gonna join you and I'm gonna have a large scotch with a *touch of water.*"

Paul, John and Simon made their way down to the bar, ordered their first drinks that they drank quickly and while waiting for their second drinks, saw two police officers approaching them.

Police officer: "Are you John, Paul and Simon from the *Time And Tide* Property?"

Paul: "We are. Why do you ask?"

Police officer: "We have been asked to come and give you these messages from Rick and Dave."

The police officer handed them two envelopes and left. John opened one letter and read out loud:

John: "We were *down on the farm* and just about to leave when *Natural Law*, the new brumby broke out of the longyard. He was *on the run* and was heading for *Good Wood* Primary School, so Dave and I gave chase in the ute. We were heading down *this road* hoping to turn the brumby towards *the valley* when a tyre blew on the ute flipping us a couple of times.
      We have both been admitted to hospital with leg and head injuries. I don't know yet how Dave is, but *I shall be released* from here as soon as I can *walk on* these crutches properly.

66

In a day or two I expect. Sorry that I missed you but you'll have to *come back soon* so we can catch up. Rick."

Simon: "This letters from Dave. He says much the same thing but he says that he'll have to spend *another Saturday night* in the hospital. His sense of humour hasn't gone 'cos he says the bang on his head had him singing the *Cloncurry Cattle song* like *the blue heeler* who backed up into a cactus plant. He says *I shall be released* next Sunday after I have learnt to *walk on* crutches without bumping into things or falling over."

Paul: "I don't know about you, but I didn't come all this way not to have contact with them. Now if these letters are real, then who were the other two guys that we spent the good part of today with?"

Simon: "I have no idea who they were, but seeing Dave has plenty of *time on his hands*, I might just stay awhile longer and visit him in hospital."

John: "I wonder if Rick is *strokin'* his *pride* back into place. He prides himself on how he doesn't mess up. The Country Music Festival is on so it won't be boring if I stay for a few more days."

Simon: "I might just stay a bit longer too, if you don't mind. Coming down I heard the *Gidgee Bug Pub* song and it's a *very good song*. Maybe they will play it somewhere down here during the festival."

Paul: "That is a *very good song*; I heard it on the bus as we were *riding into town*. At least it's different from the *Cloncurry Cattle song*. I have an open ticket so I can stay awhile longer too."

John: "We can easily get around, my Ute will carry the three of us and if I have too, I can chain Candy in the back. *This road* is good to *drive on* and if it doesn't *rock me* around too much, then Candy will be fine in the back."

They all agreed to enjoy their stay and visit Rick and Dave in hospital.

John, Simon and Paul were just about to go into the dining room, when someone came running through the back door shouting "Hey guys, a *blue heeler* has just given birth to a beautiful little pup. I wonder if her owner is in here."

John rushed outside with Paul and Simon close behind.

John: "Candy, I didn't know you were pregnant. *Back it up;* give me some room to check them both. That Dave told me this morning that Candy would have a pup, and I should call it Grace and I think I'll just do that because we thought that Candy couldn't have pups."

Paul: "Look at that unusual *ring around the moon;* I've never seen one like that before and I have spent many nights under the stars with you guys when we were on the farm and after you all left."

The waitress came out, looked up at the moon and said "I thought Earth Angel David and Angel Rick were in today. I always *carry a candle* with me and I light it so other people know that they've been here. If you fellers intend to stay around, you'll find that unusual things suddenly happen, so you had *better get used to it."*

The *shearer* said "If he has spoken to you, I hope that you listened, even if you don't understand what he said to you now, one day it'll make sense to you. Let's go in and wet the new pups head, come on let's drink. We have more beer here than *way out west."*

REFERENCE

EARTH
DUST
CARRY A CANDLE
PERPETUAL CHILD
TOUCH IN LOVE
FORGIVE AND FORGET
HANDSHAKE DEAL
THIS POOR TOWN
MY OLD FRIEND AND GENERAL LEE
THE TREE
DROWNING IN THIS DROUGHT

JAMES BLUNDELL
DANCERS
RAINBOWS
ANOTHER SATURDAY NIGHT
KIMBERLEY MOON
BANDY
A FOOL SUCH AS I
THE GREAT DIVIDE
TEXAS
CLONCURRY CATTLE SONG
PERFECT WORLD

SEA
PRIDE
HURT IS ON THE INSIDE
THE 7:45
LIBBY
DARK AGES
GUARDIAN ANGELS
BAD GIRL
HER SWEET LOVE
WALK ON
SOMETHING SACRED

TOUCH OF WATER
TOUCH OF WATER LYRICS
BRILLIANT MAN LYRICS
WALKING AWAY LYRICS
MYSTERIOUS WAYS LYRICS
SO CLOSE TO HOME LYRICS

LOAD LYRICS
IN YOUR EYES LYRICS
FAST TRAIN LYRICS
DOCTOR'S DAUGHTER LYRICS
CAN'T LOVE ALONE LYRICS
BETTER GET USED TO IT LYRICS
DREAM RIDE LYRICS
SONG FOR A HERO LYRICS
TWO TO ONE LYRICS
WEARY OF THIS WORLD LYRICS

POSTCARDS FROM SAIGON
POSTCARDS FROM SAIGON LYRICS
NATURE'S GENTLEMAN LYRICS
POSTCARDS FROM SAIGON LYRICS

RING AROUND THE MOON
LEARNING TO ROLL
FOUR FEET TALL
DRIVE ON
RING AROUND THE MOON
NATURE'S GENTLEMAN
LETS ALL GET TOGETHER (PARTY)
TOO OLD TO DIE YOUNG
THE SOUND OF YOUR SMILE
BEAUTIFUL DAY IN NEW YORK
MODERATION
THE POET AND THE QUEEN
HIGHER THAN HEAVEN
THIS IS THE TRUTH

DELUGE
FIGHT NAKED
LUNATIC FOR LOVE
POSTCARDS FROM SAIGON
GREYLANDS
ANY OTHER WAY
AIN'T GOT LOVE
24 HOUR LOVE AFFAIR
LOVE GET IN THE WAY
BE STRONG
BACK IT UP
ALL UP TO ME

70

HAND IT DOWN
AGE OF GRACE
TIME ON HIS HANDS
THE BLUE HEELER
WATER
ROCK ME
SLOW IT DOWN
HAND IT DOWN
THERE WALKS A MAN
I'M AFRAID
MEANWHILE
ACROSS THE MILES
OLD MAN

PORTRAIT OF A MAN
GOOD WOOD
RUNNING DOWN THE SUN
SHEARER
MR. RITCHIE
BOUND TO FREEZE
QUEENSLAND CALLING
FIVE TO FIVE
PORTRAIT OF A MAN
MOVING ON
NOTHING'S GOING TO GET ME DOWN
RIDING INTO TOWN
SO GOOD TO MEET YOU

THIS ROAD
THIS ROAD
DOWN ON THE FARM
YOUNG JOHN TAYLOR
THE OLD MAN'S GONE
HARD TIMES/WAY OUT WEST
I DON'T FIGHT ANYMORE
RAIN ON A TIN ROOF
ALL THAT I NEED
SHE WON'T LET YOU DOWN
CABIN FEVER
STROKIN'
OLDER NOW

I SHALL BE RELEASED: BEST OF
JAMES BLUNDELL CD
MOMENT IN TIME
OLD MANS GONE, THE
AGE OF GRACE
WALK ON
TIME ON HIS HANDS
DOWN ON THE FARM
PRIDE
VERY GOOD SONG
MYSTERIOUS WAYS
TOUCH OF WATER
RAIN ON A TIN ROOF
KIMBERLY MOON
CLONCURRY CATTLE SONG
COME BACK SOON
GUARDIAN ANGELS
VALLEY, THE
WAY OUT WEST
BLUE HEELER
THIS ROAD
I SHALL BE RELEASED

AMSTERDAM BREAKFAST
AMSTERDAM BREAKFAST
SIGNPOST
LOVE DON'T SPEAK TO ME
A VERY GOOD SONG
GREYHOUND BUSES
DYLAN, DIANA & GOD
TIME AND TIDE
ON THE RUN
NATURAL LAW
HONEY HEY
MEMORY LANE
WHO DO YOU TRUST

THE DEFINITIVE COLLECTION DVD
HIGHER THAN HEAVEN
RING AROUND THE MOON
FOUR FEET TALL
NATURE'S GENTLEMAN
POSTCARDS FROM SAIGON

DELUGE
GREYLANDS
THE VALLEY
I SHALL BE RELEASED
A VERY GOOD SONG
GUARDIAN ANGELS
PRIDE
MYSTERIOUS WAYS
WAY OUT WEST
DOWN ON THE FARM
BLUE HEELER
THIS ROAD
TIME ON HIS HANDS
AGE OF GRACE
WATER
CLONCURRY CATTLE SONG

THE ESSENTIAL
WAY OUT WEST
AGE OF GRACE
WALK ON
TIME ON HIS HANDS
DOWN ON THE FARM
RAIN ON A TIN ROOF
KIMBERLEY MOON
CLONCURRY CATTLE SONG
THE VALLEY
BLUE HEELER
THIS ROAD
THE OLD MAN'S GONE

GIDGEE BUG PUB SONG
GIDGEE BUG PUB SONG
SONG FOR LOUISE

BIBLIOGRAPHY

James Blundell picture:
http://www.jamesblundell.com.au/media/JamesBlundell004.jpg
Earth: http://listenmusic.fm/artist/James-Blundell-31054

James Blundell: http://listenmusic.fm/artist/James-Blundell-31054
Sea: http://listenmusic.fm/artist/James-Blundell-31054

Touch of Water: http://www.lyrics.com/touch-of-water-album-james-blundell.html

Postcards from Saigon:
http://www.lyrics.com/artists/albumid/james-blundell/R%20%20%20783973

Ring Around The Moon:
http://www.jamesblundell.com.au/albums.asp

Deluge: http://www.jamesblundell.com.au/albums.asp

Hand it Down: http://music.aol.com/album/hand-it-down/70086

Portrait Of A Man:
http://www.gumtreemusic.com.au/music/james-blundell/portrait-of-a-man.aspx

This Road: http://music.aol.com/album/this-road/998073

I Shall Be Released:
http://www.cduniverse.com/productinfo.asp?pid=3081621

Amsterdam Breakfast:
http://www.cduniverse.com/productinfo.asp?pid=7702816

The Definitive Collection DVD:
http://www.gumtreemusic.com.au/music/james-blundell/the-definitive-collection.aspx

The Essential:
http://901.com.au/index.php?main_page=product_info&cPath=3_4_42&products_id=1363

Gidgee Bug Pub Song:
http://www.jamesblundell.com.au/albums.asp

ADAM BRAND

FAMILY REUNION

"Mummy, mummy, Tom's just came back from town with dad's parts, before going out again and he's brought us a letter from *Uncle Pete*. Can you read it to us please?" said Alex as he handed it to his mother.

"Alright, but go get your sisters first, and then I'll only have to read it once. Susie is practicing *on Grandpa's piano* and Eve is playing her guitar down by *Senoritas* stall; you know how she loves that horse.

Tom is *eighteen,* so he can read it this evening when he is back from *Charleville.* I'll just get this last batch of Anzac biscuits out of the oven." said his mum.

Down at the stables, one of the stable hands asked Eve why she always played her guitar there, and Eve replied *"My mama told me not to play the guitar* up in the house while Susie practices on *Grandpa's piano* because she can't hear when Susie makes mistakes."

Alex went rushing up to Eve shouting "Eve, come quick, we've got a letter from *Uncle Pete* and mum's going to read it to us once you, me and Susie are together."

The children sat around the kitchen table with some of *the Anzac* biscuits that were still warm from the oven and a glass of milk each, while mum started to read the letter to them.

"Hi everyone; It's raining pretty heavy over here at the moment so I can't go to work. I thought now I finally have the time to write to you so that I wouldn't feel like I have a *wasted day* by just sitting around *waiting on sunshine. Yesterday was beautiful,* fine but not too hot.

I have made some *good friends* over here and this time of year, everyone is preparing for Christmas, and Alex, *Santa's gonna come on a surfboard.* I bet that you would like to see that.

A week before Christmas, the whole village gathers to decorate the *Blue Sky Cathedral* with *angels* and other decorations that they make themselves. I'll send you a *Christmas photo* of it. They also bring food and last year *I ate too much at Christmas.*

Every day *I thank the good Lord* that these *old hands* keep working because they're *not so strong* anymore, but *nothing's gonna slow me down.*

Eve, I ride a beautiful Bay horse named *Infinity* and I think you would love him as much as you do *Senoritas*.

I'm going to Venus Town tomorrow and I'll be sending you all a parcel, so expect something *comin' from Khe Sanh*. I'm not *beating around the bush* anymore and *words cannot say* how good it was to receive your last parcel. *The Anzac* biscuits didn't last long once my *good friends* got stuck into them. The *cigarettes & whiskey* were also appreciated as well. I hid some of the *cigarettes & whiskey* so that I would have some for myself.

You never appreciate the *good things in life, lifetime friends* and family until you receive a letter with words that *come from the heart* and my mind's made up, I'm coming home. I know I always say that after I receive parcels from you.

Blame it on Eve, for in her letter she wrote, "*Come on home* 'cos *I can't live without your love.* I want to *live right here with you*." Those words coming from a child who wears *size two boots,* will one day write the *greatest love song* of all.

Now kids, you write and tell me what you want for Christmas and don't eat all *the Anzac* biscuits before your dad and Tom get home. Eve, keep playing your guitar and Susie, you keep practicing on *Grandpa's piano,* so that you can both play me a song when I get home.

Please pass the next few pages on to Tom and the rest of the letter is for you and Steve. Hope to hear from you soon. *Uncle Pete*."

"Well." said their mum "Why don't you go and find your own place and write your letters to *Uncle Pete,* and don't forget to tell him what you want for Christmas."

In a part of his letter, Alex wrote "I had a fall from my bike and I had to have three *stitches* in my leg. I'm hoping that Santa will bring me a new *Dirt Racer* bike so that I can ride with the *Dirt Track Cowboys*. The bike that I would like is *built for speed* and will give me a *hell of a ride,* and I will also be able to ride it *here and there*.

I know that at *this time of year,* Santa's busy but *my birthday comes on Christmas* too, so a bike could be a present for both days. *When I get my wheels,* I won't be on a *losing streak* 'cos I could *get on down the road* and beat those *Dirt Track Cowboys,* even if it does seem *impossible to do*.

Dad told me that *what we do to ourselves* is *that's who we are*. I think dad meant that if I try and do my best and not give up, then I will grow up to know right from wrong and that if I want something, I'll have to work hard and save to get it and my *good friends* will want to be with me.

The Anzac biscuits that mum makes are really good, so I'll get her to make you two more batches and we'll send them with some more *cigarettes & whiskey*. Have a good Christmas, Alex."

Susie went to the dining room to write her letter and she wrote, "I am practicing to play a *gospel medley* on *Grandpa's piano*. I'm not very good at it at the moment, but I hope to be able to play it better for the next time I see you. Up there where you live, do they play or sing a *gospel medley* at Christmas in the *Blue Sky Cathedral?*

I would like a *T-Bird* jacket and a record of the group, *Get Loud* for Christmas. I think they would sound great *when the needle hits the vinyl*. Dad says that, when he plays his records on the gramophone. If I get my *Get Loud* record, I'll have to teach you to *dance with me*. *The Worm* wiggle is the new dance so I'll teach you that when you get home.

I hope the parcel *comin' from Khe Sanh* won't get lost on its way here and I hope that Santa comes to you so you can have a good Christmas. I love you. Susie."

Eve went down to the stables to write her letter. "Dear *Uncle Pete,* It was good to hear from you. I think that I would like *Infinity,* if he was anything like my horse. *My mama told me not to play the guitar* up at the house while Susie's on *Grandpa's piano* because she can't hear Susie if she makes a mistake.

I want *nuttin' for Christmas,* thank you, well, not really for myself. I believe in *angels* and *I thank the good Lord* for all the *good things in life* and I am happy with what I have already. If your *old hands* start bothering you too much, *come on home. Food water shelter love,* they're all here waiting for you if you want to come home.

It's *this time of year* when families should be together and some people make *beautiful excuses* or go *beating around the bush* to hide what *words cannot say* for them not being there.

Good friends are OK and some of them will *lie lie lie* to you but it's the *lifetime friends* that are the hardest for you to start *letting go* of when they leave.

I may just be a *little girl* but what can be *better than this* when you have a loving family around you. I *can't live without your love* and I hope that you can't live without ours. Our family could *never live without you.*

The best news you could give me, is when you tell us you're coming home; *comin' from Khe Sanh* back to us for good. Don't forget it doesn't matter, whether you are the *king of the road,* the *last man standing;* a *simple man* or the *funny little fat guy; every man likes you* for who you are but we love you more.

If I really had to choose something for myself, then *all I want for Christmas* would be you here to share it with us. I love you *Uncle Pete.* Please take care and may the good Lord watch over you. Eve."

When each child had finished their letter, they gave them to their mother for posting and then went outside to play before doing their chores.

It was after the evening meal and the kitchen had been cleaned up, Peg gave Tom his part of the letter that he took to his room to read.

"Tom, Gee, you're *eighteen* already and I bet *you're a revhead* like your father was at your age. Do you still hang around with your *good friends,* the *Dirt Track Cowboys?*

If you are a *revhead,* would you start fixing up that *big old car* of mine that's down in the shed? I used to get in it and *just drive* down to the bitumen and *get on down the road.* I used to think that I was the *king of the road,* king of the *New England Highway* and *my good friends* and I gave *Sherrif Bullfrog* a lot of trouble before he retired.

I did a lot more things in that *big old car; I* used to *love away the night,* well, part of it in the back seat. A girl I won't name, but *she's country* born, nearly got me into *trouble* and I thought that I would have to *settle down* but I'm *the lucky one* and *I thank the good Lord* for his intervention. I bet you have a *smile* on your face now.

In the parcel *coming from Khe Sanh,* will be the papers and some money to get the car on the road and when it is, *drive it till the wheels fall off.* Don't let your *dirt track cowboys* behind the wheel because they may not appreciate the *good things in life* and something *built for speed.*

I asked your brother and sisters what they wanted for Christmas and I think you're a bit old for that stuff but I still expect you to write a few lines to me and tell me if there is something that you would like.

Did you ever hear the story of some lads that went fishing down at the dam with a small amount of T.N.T.? If you haven't, then ask your dad about it 'cos *that was us* and boy when our father found out, did we get into *trouble*.

Tell your mum, in the next parcel, could she please put in three batches of *the Anzac* biscuits and tell your dad to put in a couple of bottles of *Cowboy Tequila* as well. We can get a local brand here but the Australian *Cowboy Tequila* really gets your head spinning.

I told your brother and sisters that *I'm going to Venus* Town tomorrow to post the parcel, so you can expect it in about a week's time.

That's everything I wanted to write to you about, besides *these old hands* are getting a bit tired with all this writing. Get that car of mine back on the road and don't forget that it's *built for speed* so don't get caught, especially on the *New England Highway*.

Take care and ask your dad about the dam incident and watch the *smile* come to his face. I'd like to bet that he hasn't mentioned it to you or your mum. Pete."

Tom wrote back. "*Uncle Pete,* I'll be glad to get your car back on the road for you. Dad still starts it every now and then and he also drives it *here and there* on the property. I can just imagine that it wouldn't have been hard for you, especially with those blue eyes and your smile, to *love away the night* with any female, in your car, but I'm not *ready for love* yet. There are too many things that I want to do and places that I want to travel to before I settle down.

Dad told us that you used to play the *Aussie Jingle Bells* on *Grandpa's piano* but you may not be able to play it now if your *old hands* are playing up like you said they were.

No, dad has never told us about the dam incident and I don't think that he will.

I still hang around with some of my mates from the *Dirt Track Cowboys*. I'm still at the stage where I'll *party till the money's all gone*, especially when the *Dirt Track Cowboys* and I go to the clubs in Charleville every month. We're a group of mates out for a good night out. *That's who we are* and we're going for the *good things in life* while we're still young.

I have been saving some money and hopefully in about six months' time; I'll have enough saved for a short holiday over there with you, if that's alright with you.

I'll sign off now and give this to mum to add to the other letters. Keep well and strong and I hope to see you soon. Tom."

Tom went down to the kitchen to give his letter to his mum and found her wiping tears from her eyes and asked her what was wrong.

She said "After the other children went to bed, I read their letters to find out what they wanted for Christmas and this is what Eve wrote" and handed him the letter.

After Tom had read it, he said "I have two *little sisters,* identical twins but they are both so vastly different in just about every way. Who would think this *little girl* of six years old could write this sort of letter. It really does *come from the heart,* doesn't it? There's no *beating around the bush* with her. This will really get to *Uncle Pete.* I know that *love's supposed to do* a lot of things, but this letter will stomp on his heart like someone wearing *size two boots."*

Steve, Peg's husband, came into the room interrupting the conversation. He looked at his wife's face and said "What's wrong. No bad news I hope."

Tom handed him Eve's letter and said *"Blame it on Eve.* I think that she is a true *spirit of the bush."*

Steve said *"Nah, I don't think so.* Eve, *she's country* like a lot of kids. It's *this time of year* that makes kids *crazy like that."*

Tom shook his head and replied *"Nah, I don't think so,* she is a *spirit of the bush* and that letter in your hand is *proof enough.* Read the letter dad and you'll see what I mean."

Steve read the letter and after he had finished reading it, he took a deep breath in and let it out quickly before saying *"Words cannot say* what's going through my head. The words in this letter have really *come from the heart* of a six year old. You may be right Tom, she may very well be a bush spirit and this letter is *proof enough.* It won't feel like *size two boots* that would pound his heart; it would feel more like *my boots* stomping all over it.

Fancy a kid of her age wanting *nutting for Christmas* but to see her uncle back down home with us.

Peg, should we send him this letter; you know what it'll do to him?"

Peg said "I don't know whether to send it or not. I suppose we should. Pete wrote a few pages to Tom and a few pages to us. Maybe we should read what he has to say before we decide on Eve's letter."

Tom and Peg sat down at the table while Steve put the kettle on to make a pot of tea for them. Peg started reading their part of the letter out loud.

"Steve, Peg. I've come to a decision and *my minds made up,* I'm coming home. Because my *old hands* are *not so strong* anymore, I can't continue doing the work up here. I was *stupid today* and tried to cut some timber on my own but cut my hand instead and had to have six *stitches* inserted to close the wound. There's no *beating around the bush* for me anymore and my life can be *better than this.*

Most nights I just sit around with some *good friends* and drink Cowboy Tequila until I'm *feelin' single, seeing double. I still call Australia home,* so that's where I'm heading.

It's gonna be OK because I've saved a great deal of money from working up here all these years. I'd *kinda like it* if you would allow me to bunk in with the family for a while 'till I can get settled somewhere. *You are to me* the only family where I would feel at home. I haven't heard from our other siblings since I came up here ten years ago.

Every time I read one of Eve's letters, I feel that I have an *open ended heartache* that needs to be closed.

I'm going to Venus Town tomorrow to post the parcel and it will be on its way as you read this letter, so expect the parcel to arrive soon. In the parcel are the papers for my old car and some money to get it on the road. Steve, *you're a revhead* or you used to be, so I expect your son is the same.

If you could get the children's letters in the post within the next day or two, then I'll know what to get them for Christmas; that is if you haven't got them already.

The *stitches* in my hand come out next week and then it will take me another three days to get to the big city for a flight home, so I should be there a day or two before Christmas. I will ring you when I get into Sydney. This is one time when *nothin's gonna slow me down,* not even if I'm the *last man standing* wearing size two boots.

Steve and Peg, I could *never live without you* being there for me when I needed someone. Please don't tell the children that I'm coming home as I want to surprise them. See you in a few weeks and Peg; get cracking on *the Anzac* biscuits. Pete."

Steve said as he poured the tea "Well *that changes everything.* We have to send him Eve's letter now, seeing he's coming home.

I'm *wondering* if he'd like to stay with us and work on the property. I know that there'll be enough work for him to do that he'll be able to do, or do you think that he'll want to get a place and job of his own? Peg, Tom what do you think?"

Tom answered his father by saying "A place of his own, *Nah, I don't think so.* I think that once he gets here, he'll never want to leave.

Uncle Pete said in his letter to me that his car was *built for speed* and that you and him with some of your mates used to *get on down the road* and down the *New England Highway.*

He also said that you and him went fishing in the dam with T.N.T. You didn't tell me that story, so what gives?"

Steve said "He said *I did what?"*

Tom said "Come on dad, I know that something went down by that *smile* on your face and Uncle Pete said to watch your face for the smile."

Peg said "You haven't told me that story so you'd better tell me your version now because we're bound to hear Pete's version when he gets here."

Steve told them the story and he ended it by saying, "Yep *that was us.*"

Tom said "Mum if you can write a reply to your part of the letter tonight, I'll post them tomorrow when I get to *Charleville.*

I don't really feel like going now, but the *Dirt Track Cowboys* are expecting me to take some of them in for the night. Randy can't fit them all in his van. I would sooner stay here and work on the car."

Peg's answer to her part of the letter was "Pete, We're so glad that you're coming home. You know that you are welcome to stay with us for as long as you want or need to. *Food water shelter love* all wait for you here. You won't have to drink at night unless you're *feelin' single, seeing double* although you will think that you're seeing double when you see the girls. We could *never live without you* too.

Tom has been given a new lease on his young life and can't wait to get started on your car. There is *nothing like a good day* and your letter has made mine a very good day.

No, we don't have any Christmas presents at the moment and you don't have to buy the children what they want. We're really *getting good at living life* the simple way. *That's who we are* and nothing is going to change that. Having you home for Christmas will be a welcome present for all of us especially being *right here with you* in person.

The Anzac biscuits are not a problem as I make them all the time; they are the family's favourite biscuits.

I'll be waiting for your phone call when you get in to Sydney and we will make some arrangements on picking you up. Either Tom or Steve will come and get you. Hope your hand doesn't bother you too much." Love Peg.

The following weeks were busy, getting things ready for Christmas and *Uncle Pete's* homecoming. It was hard to keep the latter from the younger children because they had to clean out and prepare the spare room without them thinking too much about what we were doing. Conversations were also suddenly stopped when one of the younger children wandered past.

The parcel arrived with a few things for the family and the papers and money for the car. In the parcel was a pair of riding boots, made by the *Size Two Boots* Company, for Eve, some sheets of music to play on *Grandpa's piano* for Susie, a set of cooking bowls for Peg, a shirt each for Alex and Tom and a record, *Unafraid To Love I Surrender* made by the local village band, *Last Man Standing* for Steve.

Steve was not impressed by the gift but the *Dirt Track Cowboys* liked it and played it over and over again until Peg said *"One more time tonight and that's it. You can turn it off and go outside."* But *when the needle hits the vinyl,* care should be taken because a *thump* could cause the needle to jump or slide across the record scratching it. And that's just what happened as the *Dirt Track Cowboys* were playing around, the record got scratched.

Tom said, just as his father walked into the room "Oh no. Now we're in *T.R.O.U.B.L.E.*"

Steve said "In trouble for what?"

Tom showed the scratched record to his father and said "Sorry dad, *that was us, the bug,* pointing to one of the *Dirt Track Cowboys,* was messing around with me and we were too close the gramophone."

Bug said *"I did what?"*

Steve looked at each one of the boys and said *"It's gonna be OK.* Pete can always get one of the *Last Man Standing* band members to send us another copy. I don't think that it would be *impossible to do,* seeing they're the local village band who made it.

How's the car going? Have you taken it out on the *New England Highway* yet, for a test drive?"

Tom replied "No, we haven't. I didn't think that you would allow me to drive it out on the highway."

"Well, that's what Pete wanted you to do; although I'm not too happy about it, but only you are allowed to *just drive* it at all times. As this will your first time driving it on the *New England Highway;* remember, it's *built for speed* and you are not *the king of the road* or the *last man standing. This time of year,* there will be more traffic on the roads due to the holiday makers and more patrol cars."

Peg walked up to Steve, as the boys walked outside and said "Do you think that he'll listen to you?"

Steve looked at Peg and said *"Nah, I don't think so,* that car was *built for speed* and once they *get on down the road* and find a deserted stretch of the *New England Highway,* they'll open it up a bit.

Tom's not a stupid driver; he won't take any unnecessary chances even if the other guys do start egging him on to do stuff."

The boys were gone for a couple of hours and when they returned, Tom said "That car really was *built for speed,* wasn't it. I only did the speed limit on the *New England Highway* and didn't pretend to be the *king of the road. Someday, when I get my wheels,* I'd like to do it up and have it running like that car."

Steve had a chuckle to himself before saying "*You're a revhead,* just like Pete and I were when we first got that car. It gave us a *hell of a ride* many times. Many nights, Pete attempted to *love away the night* in its back seat. More often than not, he was on a *losing streak* because there was no *beating around the bush* with the girls back then. They weren't interested in that sort of thing until they got married."

A sudden clanging and banging noise and shouting were heard coming from the stables and Steve said to Tom "Go and see what all that commotion is about. Your *little sisters* are up to something? It must be them as I just saw them from the window going in there."

Tom hurried into the stable and saw four buckets scattered on the floor and Susie sitting over Eve, who was pinned to the ground.

Tom asked "What are you two up to? Did you knock these buckets over?"
Eve said as she was getting up "Sorry, *that was us,* it was an accident."

Tom looked at the girls and asked "Were you fighting again and what were you fighting over?"

Eve said "I heard and saw Susie *kissing the phone* so I started to tease her about it."

Susie shouted "*I did what?*"

Eve smartly replied "You were kissing the phone but did it *kiss you back?*"

Susie got up and stomped out of the stables saying "*You are to me* the biggest pain. Why don't you *get your gear off* and go jump in the dam and forget to come out. I'm going to practice my *Gospel Melody* on *Grandpa's piano.*"

Steve went running up to the stables as Susie was stomping out and said "What happened here? Is everything alright?"

Susie just said *"Blame it on Eve."* and just kept going; walking towards the house.

Tom walked out shaking his head, smiling and said *"Little sisters, fighting over nothing as per usual."*

Two days before Christmas, Susie and Eve were helping their mother in the kitchen preparing the food for the big day. Alex and his father were cleaning up the veranda and the yard for where the celebrations were going to be held and Tom washed and polished the car, did a few extra chores at the stables and then made sure Pete's room was ready for him when he arrived.

After Tom had finished upstairs, he went to the kitchen for a drink and said to Susie "It smells good in here. What have you been cooking?"

Susie replied *"We're makin' up* extra biscuits, scones and cakes because mum says that you never know who will drop in and see us and we're nearly finished."

Tom walked over to the warm scones and took one and said "There's *nothing like a good day cooking* for everybody. It's one of the *good things in life* that we all share together. *Every man likes you* females after you've been cooking yummy food."

Susie looked at her big brother in disgust and said "Well, *that changes everything;* if that's all I can look forward to when I grow up, then I'm going to stop cooking. I want to play the piano all over the world and not just *here and there* after spending my time just cooking and cleaning. I don't need the look of *old hands* when I'm playing the piano."

"We've finished and cleaned up in here, so can we go and play now mum?" said Eve.

"Yes, and thank you for your help." said their mum.

As the girls left the kitchen, Peg said "Tom is everything ready for Pete? Your father and I were talking last night and we think that it would be nice for you to pick up Pete in his car once he's phoned us and told us where he is."

"That sounds like a good idea. I'm sure that once I *get on down the road,* it won't take long for me to get him back here and the younger children won't suspect anything. They'll just think that I've gone to see some *good friends* down the road on the neighbouring farm." said Tom.

Down at the stables, one of the stable hands walked up to Eve and said "There's been a nice smell coming from the house. Has your mother been baking again?"

Eve looked at him and said *"That was us;* mum, Susie and me cooking. *My mum and Santa* made a deal when I was little, she would bake and leave something out for him and his reindeers and he would make sure that his reindeers would not mess up the yard. I think that we also made enough to share with everyone here."

The following day being the day before Christmas, the children were all up early and had their chores done quickly and were off playing on their own. Eve was down at the stable as that's where she usually spent most of her time, Susie was outback sitting under a tree reading her music book and Alex was riding his old bike down the drive beside the house, when he spotted a horse drawn wagon coming up the road towards the house.

He went rushing inside to his mother shouting excitedly, "Mum come quick, *here comes Santa Claus* up our road in a wagon with horses pulling it instead of his reindeer."

Just as the man halted the wagon, he got down and said "I have a special and early delivery for *number 34.* Am I at the right place?"

Peg said "Yes you are."

Meanwhile, except for Eve, the rest of the family and stable hands had gathered around the wagon that had five boxes of varying sizes on it.

"I was told that you were expecting these. Please sign here." and I was to give you this and the man handed Peg a letter.

Once the goods were unloaded from the wagon and placed on the veranda, Peg opened the letter and read "These gifts come in two parts, the first part you now have, so please enjoy them now and not tomorrow."

Peg looked at Steve and said "Why not. Thank you boys for helping to unload the wagon, you can go back to what you were doing." and proceeded to indicate which box belonged to whom.

Meanwhile, still down at the stables, Eve was looking down and playing her guitar when she heard a man say "Why do you play on your own down here?"

Thinking it was one of the stable hands, she said "You know why; *my mama told me not to play the guitar* up at the house." and then looked up to see a strange man with a wrapped gift for her in his hand offering her to take it.

Normally Eve would not talk to any stranger but would call for someone, but something inside her told her that she was not in any danger from this man but to trust him and accept his gift.

He said to her "When they *come from the heart, words cannot say* anything but the truth and you speak the truth and there's no *beating around the bush* when you do. You really do believe that the *good things in life* come from your family. This is a very special gift for a very special someone who wanted nothing for herself for Christmas.

Many people during your lifetime will *never live without you,* your love or your help. Some people will *love away the night* after you have touched their lives in a certain way. You will never be on a *losing streak* and you will close an *open ended heartache* tonight. You will make many people happy tonight in more ways than one.

Now Eve, I know that you will not remember the words or understand what I have said to you today, but as you grow up and things happen to you and around you, you will. Now go up to the house with the rest of your family and share in their happiness and please, light *one candle* for me, just *one more time tonight*."

Eve took the wrapped gift and watched as the stranger walk out of the stable door and then she raced up to the house, getting there just in time to see Susie finish opening her box and start pulling out its contents.

Look mum she said excitedly "Look, *Get Loud* records. I think that these must be every *Get Loud* record that they have made. There are six records here. And look, I have got the *T-Bird* jacket that I really wanted as well as everything else to do with them.

There's a note too and it says "I hope you like these gifts. Another surprise is coming for you and you will have it by tomorrow. Have a Merry Christmas."

Alex opened his box and stood there staring at it for a minute, like he couldn't believe his eyes.

His father said "What have you got in your box Alex?"

Alex replied "A *Dirt Racer* bike and all the accessories." as he pulled it out of the box. "This must be the best *Dirt Racer* bike that they make. Now I can be a real *Dirt Track Cowboy*. There are also some board games in here that I can play with you all. There's *Beating Around The Bush,* The *Last Man Standing* and *Scrabble.*

I have a note too and it says "Once you have mastered your bike, you will easily beat all the *Dirt Track Cowboys* for years to come. The best game to play will be The *Last Man Standing*. Your other surprise is coming and you will also have it by tomorrow. Have a Merry Christmas."

Tom opened his medium sized box to find the most up to date tool box and tool kit along with several pairs of overalls. He also found a gramophone of his own, four spare needles and two copies of his fathers scratched record by *Last Man Standing* band.

Tom said "A complete tool kit for *when I get my wheels*. Hey dad, Tom held up both records; one for you and one for me.

My note says, "You will have your wheels sooner than you think. Don't try to *love away the night* in it too soon as you will not be *ready for love* for another four years yet. You have extra needles and an extra record just in case your mates scratch the other one."

Peg opened her box and saw a brand new, latest model washing machine. Sitting on the top of the washer were two smaller boxes. One box contained the blue cotton dress that she had often seen in the dress shop window when she was in town but could never afford and the other box held a large bottle of her favourite perfume, Heaven Sent, that she was almost out of.

Her note read "The *good things in life* are sometimes given as a special thank you to a person who deserves it. Wear your new dress and perfume tomorrow, for your family *can't live without your love* and they do appreciate you even if they don't show or tell you. Have a Merry Christmas."

Steve opened his box to find a portable petrol driven generator, the latest petrol powered chain saw, two new pairs of jeans, two new shirts and three new mixed country records of his favourite artists.

His note read "*Blame it on Eve. She's country* and is a true *spirit of the bush*. Her love and her faith come from you and you have instilled in her the true meaning of the *good things in life. What we do to ourselves* is also what we do to and for our children. You should be very proud of all of them as well as your lovely wife and yourself. Have a Merry Christmas."

There was one smaller box left to open and it had Eve's name on it.

Alex looked around and saw Eve standing back with the unwrapped present in her hand and said "Come on open your box. What have you got there in your hand and where did you get it from?"

Eve walked over to her box and carefully put the other present down. When she opened her box, she found a really pretty pink dress and matching shoes inside as well as some new riding clothes and a new saddle.

She opened her note and read it out loud "Wear the dress and shoes tomorrow. Pink is the angel's colour of love. Enjoy riding your horse because both of you will enjoy the peace of the bush for years to come. *Some dreams* for special people do come true, so turn around for yours is about to come true. Have a Merry Christmas."

Eve and the rest of her family turned around to see a man walking up to the house carrying a small suitcase.

"Uncle Pete." cried Eve and rushed down to greet him, with everyone else following her and forgetting about her other present.

Half an hour later, after everyone had said their greetings and Pete had settled in, everyone was sitting around the table with a cup of tea.
Peg said "Pete, I thought that you were going to ring us when you got off the plane in Sydney?"

Pete's reply was "Two days ago, in the village where I was living, there was an unusual monsoonal downpour; so bad that I didn't think that I would get out of there on the bus later that day.

One of the villager's relatives was heading back to the big city and asked me if I wanted to go with him, so I did. We were half way down the mountain, when a landslide happened and block the road behind us.

I was driven straight to the airport and when I went to book and pay for my ticket on the next flight out, I was informed that my ticket had already been paid for and that they were holding the plane because they knew my arrival would be delayed by a few minutes. I was also informed that there would be someone waiting for me at Sydney airport. I thought that it may have been either you, Steve or Tom.

We arrived in Sydney fifteen minutes early and sure enough, there was this man waiting for me. I thought that I had either seen or met this man before but I couldn't remember where.

He approached me and asked me to go with him and I thought he may have been someone to do with customs, so I went with him but instead of going to customs, he took me straight outside to a waiting taxi. My luggage was being placed into the boot and the driver was standing by the opened back door.

The man who had greeted me never told me his name, but as I got into the taxi, he handed me an envelope and told me that the driver knew where to take me and the fare had been paid. As the driver closed the door, I heard the man say "Now *that's a man* who is *waiting on sunshine*."

In the taxi, I opened the envelope to find five hundred Australian dollars, mostly fifty and twenty dollar notes, a bus ticket and this note; he pulled the note out of his pocket and proceeded to read it "You can *blame it on Eve,* for without her, the *good things in life* wouldn't be so good. Now *we're making up* for many lost years that you have had.

Truthful words that *come from the heart* cannot be ignored, not even by the *last man standing*. Your *open ended heartache* will now be closed forever and now *that changes everything* else to do with the rest of your life. Within six months, your *old hands* will be a lot better and being back *down home* where you belong will make a difference to you.

Eve, *she's country* but she will meet a *simple man,* like her father, when she grows up and *what a life* they will have with their children. She will remember everything that she has been taught and that will also be reflected in her children, especially her son.

Susie will never have a *wasted day* while playing the piano on tour in many countries. She will also be an inspiration for other less fortunate children and will also end up teaching them.

Alex will be a lot like you and will make a living working *here and there*. He too will travel but will never forget where home is. He will eventually settle down overseas with a very good woman and in a company that will also benefit your whole family.

Tom will become the *king of the road* with the products of your farm that he will transport. He will have many dealings with Alex and they will form a very viable and healthy export business. Have a Merry Christmas."

The taxi driver had no trouble getting me to the Greyhound Bus station because there wasn't any traffic on the road which was very, very unusual because we came across the Sydney Harbour Bridge.

At the bus station, my cases were put straight on to the bus and like the plane, they were waiting for me. I must have dozed off for a while as we were travelling up the highway and the driver woke me by saying "*Number 34*, that's where your family live, don't they?" as he suddenly pulled over and stopped the bus right in front of your house.

As he took my little suitcase out of the luggage compartment he told me that the rest of my luggage would be up at the house waiting for me. I never had time to do anything, that's why I didn't phone you to let you know that I'd arrived.

These past two days have seemed like I'm living in this weird dream.

There was a knock on the back door and when Tom opened it, he saw Pete's other luggage just sitting on the door step but no other person was insight.

"Let's not worry about that now." said Peg. "Let's all have a good night's sleep and we'll sort it out tomorrow. It has been a very exciting and confusing day for us all."

Christmas morning arrived and everyone was up early, especially the younger children who found other presents under the Christmas tree.

Peg called Pete into the kitchen and said "Pete, thank you for the presents that were delivered by wagon yesterday but please tell me; how did you know that I needed a new washing machine and that I have been admiring this dress for months now. You shouldn't have been so extravagant in buying the gifts."

Pete looked confused at her and said "*I did what?*"

Peg looked at him and replied "Stop *beating around the bush*. Didn't you ask the children what they wanted for Christmas, and what they asked for, was delivered yesterday, including a tool kit, overalls, a gramophone and records for Tom, a portable generator and chainsaw and clothes for Steve and my gifts."

Pete said "I told you yesterday what happened to me and I swear to you, I haven't bought anything for any of the family except what I placed under the tree last night."

"But what about all those notes that we got with the presents? The notes told the younger children, you were coming home as a surprise for all of us but it wasn't mentioned in Tom's, Steve's or my notes because we knew you were coming. So did you arrange for someone else to do it?" asked Peg.

"No." said Pete. "Who could I get to do it? I've been out of the country for the past ten years and I haven't kept in touch with anyone except you and Steve. There weren't any other Aussies near to where I was working that I could get to do it for me either."

"Well, someone certainly came because Eve came back from the stables with a wrapped present in her hand that someone had given to her." Peg said anxiously.

Pete said "Let's not panic. Let's go and open the other presents and we'll let Eve tell us who gave her that present down at the stables."

Pete and Peg went back into the living room where there were three excited children waiting to open their presents and as Pete walked past Tom, Tom said "*owyagoin' Santa Claus.*"

This time it was Tom who received the special present, Pete's old car. Pete told Tom that he didn't feel safe driving it and him being young, it would be better for him.

Pete finished by saying "*You're a revhead,* so make good use of it, except don't try to *love away the night* in the back seat 'cos it don't work. You only end up on a *losing streak.* I've thought about this very carefully and came to the decision to give you the car; that is if you want it. When *my mind's made up, my mind's made up* and I don't change it."

94

Steve chose one of his new country records and put it on the gramophone and said "Listen to that, *when the needle hits the vinyl,* the sound is so clear."

Pete called the girl's names and as they turned and looked at him, he said "Your mother was right; she said that when I look at you two it would be like me *feelin' single, seein' double.* Now Susie, how about you play me something on *Grandpa's piano* and then Eve, you play me something on your guitar."

Eve said "*My mama told me not to play the guitar* up here in the house."

Pete said "I think that an exception can be made for today. Don't you think so Peg?"

He then turned to Steve and said "Steve remember back to when *you're a revhead* and these *old hands* were playing the piano; you came in and started playing with me and you greased up the keys and mum really got mad at us."

"*I did what?*" said Steve.

Pete said "Come now, you know what I'm talking about. I know you do by the *smile* on your face?"

Alex said "Anyone wanna play The *Last Man Standing* with me?"

Tom said "This afternoon, after lunch, I'll have a game with you."

Peg said "Eve, yesterday, you came up from the stables with a wrapped gift in your hand. What was it and where did it come from?"

Eve answered her mother by saying "I don't know what it is, when I saw Uncle Pete coming I forgot all about it. It's still outside; I'll go and get it."

Eve came back in with the gift in one hand and another gift for her uncle in the other hand.

"Uncle Pete, this gift was left next to this one and it's got your name on it." said Eve and handed him the gift.

Pete ripped the paper off and started laughing, then called Steve over and showed him and Steve started laughing too.

Pete turned the frame around and showed the rest of the family a photo of the pair of them, in the kitchen of their old home, covered in chocolate cake and chocolate icing.

Susie asked "Dad, is that you and Uncle Pete?"

Steve said "Yes *that was us* when we were young." then he said to Pete "I wonder where this came from. I don't remember anyone taking a photo of us."

Pete, trying to contain his laughter said "*That was us* when we were ten years old, after mum told us to share what was left of the chocolate cake mix. Can you remember what she said when she saw us and her messy kitchen?"

"No." said Steve.

"I didn't think so 'cos you took off to the dam saying "I'm outta here and *nothin's gonna slow me down*." and went flying out the back door." said Pete.

"*I did what?* It was you who took off, but didn't we cop it from mum when we both got home." said Steve.

They both laughed again.

Peg looked at her three young children sitting on the floor and said "I had better start watching my chocolate cake mixes from now on and don't you children get any ideas."

Eve un-wrapped her forgotten present and said "Mum look at this beautiful angel. It is just like the man who gave it to me." and then she turned the statue around for everyone else to see.

Alex looked at the statue and quickly turned to his mother saying "Mum, that's the man who brought us those boxes yesterday."

Susie said "It is the man, mum. I saw his really nice blue eyes and he had a nice smile as well."

Pete exclaimed "It can't be. He's the man who met me at the Sydney airport. Hang on a moment."

Pete got out of the chair and disappeared upstairs. When he came back down a few minutes later; he had two photos in his hand. He looked at the statue, then at the photos and back to the statue and said "I thought I'd seen the man who greeted me at the airport before and turned the photos around.

Tom said after examining both the photos and the statue "The photos do look kinda like it. Who is he?"

Pete explained "Back in the village where I was living, the people called him THIZN SU CUA TRAI DAT DAVID, translated means Earth Angel David. The villagers believed that he would visit someone in need, or answer someone's prayer and sometimes make the dreams of someone special come true."

Pete paused for a moment then continued "Now, *that changes everything* and answers the questions I keep asking myself. Eve, did he speak to you?"

"Yes." said Eve "After I had finished brushing Senoritas and telling her that *life will bring you home* to us because we could *never live without you,* but I can't remember what he said. He told me that I wouldn't remember now but as I grow up, things will happen and I will remember then. Why, did I do something wrong?"

Pete gave her a hug and softly said "No, you didn't do or say anything wrong. *Words cannot say* what *you are to me,* what all of *you are to me.* In fact; if you want to know *the reason I come home,* well, she's right here. *Blame it on Eve.*"

Peg said "Anyone for *Anzac* biscuits, cake, scones and a cup of tea?"

The family said "Yes please." and went out to the kitchen to get some goodies.

REFERENCE

ADAM BRAND
UNCLE PETE
NEVER LIVE WITHOUT YOU
GRANDPA'S PIANO
MY MINDS MADE UP
COME FROM THE HEART
FEELIN' SINGLE, SEEIN' DOUBLE
LOSING STREAK
LAST MAN STANDING
SIZE TWO BOOTS
DIRT TRACK COWBOYS
MY MAMA TOLD ME (NOT TO PLAY THE GUITAR)
HERE AND THERE
KING OF THE ROAD
WORDS CANNOT SAY
LOVE AWAY THE NIGHT
GOSPEL MELODY
CHARLEVILLE
TROUBLE

BLAME IT ON EVE
GET ON DOWN THE ROAD
PROOF ENOUGH
BLAME IT ON EVE
NOTHING LIKE A GOOD DAY
COMIN' FROM / KHE SANH
NOT SO STRONG
DOWN HOME
WASTED DAY
BETTER THAN THIS
WAITING ON SUNSHINE
SIMPLE MAN
WHAT WE DO TO OURSELVES
RIGHT HERE WITH YOU
ANGELS
SPIRIT OF THE BUSH (LEE KERNAGHAN AND STEVE FORDE) -
BONUS TRACK

ADAM BRAND - BLAME IT ON EVE LIMITED EDITION (CD AND DVD)
DISC 1:
GET ON DOWN THE ROAD
PROOF ENOUGH
BLAME IT ON EVE
NOTHING LIKE A GOOD DAY
COMIN' FROM / KHE SANH
NOT SO STRONG
DOWN HOME
WASTED DAY
BETTER THAN THIS
WAITING ON SUNSHINE
SIMPLE MAN
WHAT WE DO TO OURSELVES
RIGHT HERE WITH YOU
ANGELS
SPIRIT OF THE BUSH - FEAT. LEE KERNAGHAN & STEVE FORDE - (BONUS TRACK)
DISC 2:
MIN 'MAKING OF' DOCUMENTARY (NOT USED IN STORY)
GET ON DOWN THE ROAD - (VIDEO)

HELL OF A RIDE CD
HELL OF A RIDE
KISSING THE PHONE
WONDERING
READY FOR LOVE
BLUE SKY CATHEDRAL
CRAZY LIKE THAT
THAT'S A MAN
THUMP
SOME DREAMS
LETTING GO
STUPID TODAY
YESTERDAY WAS BEAUTIFUL

BUILT FOR SPEED
NEW ENGLAND HIGHWAY
I'M GOING TO VENUS
THE ANZAC
THAT WAS US
DIRT RACER

THAT'S WHO WE ARE
BUILT FOR SPEED
NOTHING'S GONNA SLOW ME DOWN
OLD HANDS
I THANK THE GOOD LORD
SMILE
NAH, I DON'T THINK SO
STITCHES

GET LOUD
WE'RE MAKIN' UP
INFINITY
GET LOUD
NUMBER 34
THIS TIME OF YEAR
FOOD WATER SHELTER LOVE
EIGHTEEN
COWBOY TEQUILA
IMPOSSIBLE TO DO
LIFETIME FRIENDS
JUST DRIVE
SENORITAS
COME ON HOME
SHE'S COUNTRY

GOOD FRIENDS
BIG OLD CAR
WHEN THE NEEDLE HITS THE VINYL
GOOD FRIENDS
YOU ARE TO ME
I DID WHAT?
BEATING AROUND THE BUSH
LITTLE SISTERS
GOOD THINGS IN LIFE
WHEN I GET MY WHEELS
LITTLE GIRL
EVERY MAN LIKES YOU
YOU'RE A REVHEAD
ONE MORE TIME TONIGHT

WHAT A LIFE (2006)
CAN'T LIVE WITHOUT YOUR LOVE LYRICS
CIGARETTES & WHISKY LYRICS

DRIVE IT TILL THE WHEELS FALL OFF LYRICS
KINDA LIKE IT LYRICS
LIFE WILL BRING YOU HOME LYRICS
MY BOOTS LYRICS
OPEN ENDED HEARTACHE LYRICS
PARTY TILL THE MONEY'S ALL GONE LYRICS
SETTLE DOWN LYRICS
THAT CHANGES EVERYTHING LYRICS
THE BUG LYRICS
THE LUCKY ONE LYRICS
WHAT A LIFE LYRICS

ADAM BRAND (1998)
ADAM BRAND - BONUS LIVE TRACKS: LYRICS
ADAM BRAND - CHARLEVILLE LYRICS
ADAM BRAND - COME FROM THE HEART LYRICS
ADAM BRAND - DIRT TRACK COWBOYS LYRICS
ADAM BRAND - FEELIN' SINGLE, SEEIN' DOUBLE LYRICS
ADAM BRAND - GOSPEL MEDLEY LYRICS
ADAM BRAND - GRANDPA'S PIANO LYRICS
ADAM BRAND - HERE AND THERE LYRICS
ADAM BRAND - KING OF THE ROAD LYRICS
ADAM BRAND - LAST MAN STANDING LYRICS
LOSING STREAK LYRICS
LOVE AWAY THE NIGHT LYRICS
MY MAMA TOLD ME (NOT TO PLAY THE GUITAR) LYRICS
MY MINDS MADE UP LYRICS
NEVER LIVE WITHOUT YOU LYRICS
SIZE TWO BOOTS LYRICS
T-BIRD LYRICS
TROUBLE LYRICS
UNCLE PETE LYRICS
WORDS CANNOT SAY LYRICS

CHRISTMAS IN AUSTRALIA (2005)
ALL I WANT FOR CHRISTMAS (IS MY TWO FRONT TEETH)
LYRICS
ATE TOO MUCH AT CHRISTMAS LYRICS
AUSSIE JINGLE BELLS LYRICS
BUILT FOR SPEED LYRICS
CHRISTMAS PHOTO LYRICS
DIRT TRACK COWBOYS LYRICS
FUNNY LITTLE FAT GUY LYRICS

GET YOUR GEAR OFF LYRICS
GOOD THINGS IN LIFE LYRICS
HERE COMES SANTA CLAUS LYRICS
LAST MAN STANDING LYRICS
MY BIRTHDAY COMES ON CHRISTMAS LYRICS
MY MUM AND SANTA LYRICS
NEW ENGLAND HIGHWAY LYRICS
NUTTIN' FOR CHRISTMAS LYRICS
OLD HANDS LYRICS
ONE CANDLE LYRICS
OWYAGOIN' SANTA CLAUS LYRICS
SANTA'S GONNA COME ON A SURFBOARD LYRICS
THAT WAS US LYRICS
UNCLE PETE LYRICS

IT'S GONNA BE OK CD
IT'S GONNA BE OK
KISS YOU BACK
DANCE WITH ME THE WORM
UNAFRAID TO LOVE I SURRENDER
THE REASON I COME HOME
GETTING' GOOD AT LIVING LIFE
GREATEST LOVE SONG
LOVE'S SUPPOSED TO DO
LIE LIE LIE
THAT'S EVERYTHING
BEAUTIFUL EXCUSES

GOOD FRIENDS; GET LOUD
DISC 1: GOOD FRIENDS
BIG OLD CAR
WHEN THE NEEDLE HITS THE VINYL
GOOD FRIENDS
YOU ARE TO ME
I DID WHAT
BEATING AROUND THE BUSH
LITTLE SISTERS
GOOD THINGS IN LIFE
WHEN I GET MY WHEELS
LITTLE GIRL
EVERY MAN LIKES YOU
YOU'RE A REVHEAD
ONE MORE TIME TONIGHT

DISC 2: GET LOUD
WE'RE MAKIN' UP
INFINITY
GET LOUD
NUMBER 34
THIS TIME OF YEAR
FOOD WATER SHELTER LOVE
EIGHTEEN
COWBOY TEQUILA
IMPOSSIBLE TO DO
LIFETIME FRIENDS
JUST DRIVE
SENORITAS
COME ON HOME
SHE'S COUNTRY
DOCUMENTARY VIDEO (BONUS) (NOT USED IN STORY)

ADAM BRAND/BUILT FOR SPEED
UNCLE PETE
NEVER LIVE WITHOUT YOU
GRANDPA'S PIANO
MY MIND'S MADE UP
COME FROM THE HEART
FEELIN' SINGLE SEEIN' DOUBLE
LOSING STREAK
LAST MAN STANDING
SIZE TWO BOOTS
DIRT TRACK COWBOYS
MY MAMA TOLD ME (NOT TO PLAY THE GUITAR)
HEAR AND THERE
KING OF THE ROAD
WORDS CANNOT SAY
LOVE AWAY THE NIGHT
GOSPEL MEDLEY
UNCLE PETE (LIVE)
CHARLEVILLE (LIVE)
NEVER LIVE WITHOUT YOU (LIVE)
SIZE TWO BOOTS (LIVE)
T BIRD (LIVE)
T-R-O-U-B-L-E (LIVE)
NEW ENGLAND HIGHWAY
I'M GOING TO VENUS
ANZAC

THAT WAS US
DIRT RACER
THAT'S WHO WE ARE
BUILT FOR SPEED
NOTHIN' GONNA SLOW ME DOWN
OLD HANDS
I THANK THE GOOD LORD
SMILE
NAH, I DON'T THINK SO
STITCHES
NEW ENGLAND HIGHWAY
I'M GOING TO VENUS
THE ANZAC
THAT WAS US
DIRT RACER
THAT'S WHO WE ARE
BUILT FOR SPEED
NOTHIN'S GONNA SLOW ME DOWN
OLD HANDS
I THANK THE GOOD LORD
SMILE
NAH, I DON'T THINK SO
STITCHES

ADAM BRAND
COMIN' FROM / KHE SANH
READY FOR LOVE
ITS GONNA BE OK
HELL OF A RIDE
LEE KERNAGHAN, ADAM BRAND & STEVE FORDE- SPIRIT OF
THE BUSH - MUSIC VIDEO
THE ANZAC
BEATING AROUND THE BUSH
WORDS CANNOT SAY
I DID WHAT
YOU ARE TO ME ADAM BRAND
YOUR A REVHEAD
GET ON DOWN THE ROAD
BLUE SKY CATHEDRAL
THIS TIME OF YEAR
THAT CHANGES EVERYTHING
NUTTIN' FOR CHRISTMAS

THE SUNNY COWGIRLS FEATURING ADAM BRAND –
SOMEDAY
ADAM BRAND AT HTTP:WWW.KIDSOLO.COM (NOT USED IN
STORY)
BLAME IT ON EVE
GOOD THINGS IN LIFE

ADAM BRAND - GREATEST HITS 1998 - 2008 CD
LAST MAN STANDING
GRANPA'S PIANO
DIRT TRACK COWBOYS
GOOD FRIENDS
BEATING AROUND THE BUSH
GOOD THINGS IN LIFE
I DID WHAT?
NEW ENGLAND HIGHWAY
THE ANZAC
THAT WAS US
OLD HANDS
GET LOUD
SHE'S COUNTRY
THIS TIME OF YEAR
OPEN ENDED HEARTACHE
CAN'T LIVE WITHOUT YOUR LOVE
CIGARETTES & WHISKEY
THAT CHANGES EVERYTHING
BLAME IT ON EVE (ACOUSTIC) (BONUS TRACK)
DIRT TRACK COWBOYS 08 (BONUS TRACK)

GREATEST HITS 1998-2008 DVD
LAST MAN STANDING
GRANDPA'S PIANO
DIRT TRACK COWBOY
LOVE AWAY THE NIGHT (FEAT. MELINDA SCHNEIDER)
GOOD FRIENDS
BEATING AROUND THE BUSH
GOOD THINGS IN LIFE (LIVE)
I DID WHAT
BUILT FOR SPEED (LIVE)
NEW ENGLAND HIGHWAY (LIVE)
THAT WAS US (LIVE)
THE ANZAC
OLD HANDS

GET LOUD
SHE'S COUNTRY
THIS TIME OF YEAR
OPEN ENDED HEARTACHE
CAN'T LIVE WITHOUT YOUR LOVE
CIGARETTES & WHISKEY
THAT CHANGES EVERYTHING
GET ON DOWN THE ROAD
COMING FROM/KHE SANH
BLAME IT ON EVE
BLAME IT ON EVE (BONUS FOOTAGE - ACOUSTIC)

ADAM BRAND - BUILT FOR SPEED - LIVE IN CONCERT DVD
UNCLE PETE (LIVE VIDEO VERSION)
LAST MAN STANDING (LIVE VIDEO VERSION)
OLD HANDS (LIVE VIDEO VERSION)
GRANDPA'S PIANO (LIVE VIDEO VERSION)
THAT WAS US (LIVE VIDEO VERSION)
GOOD THINGS IN LIFE (LIVE VIDEO VERSION)
NAH, I DON'T THINK SO (LIVE VIDEO VERSION)
BUILT FOR SPEED (LIVE VIDEO VERSION)
YOU'RE A REVHEAD (LIVE VIDEO VERSION)
SMILE (LIVE VIDEO VERSION)
NEW ENGLAND HIGHWAY (LIVE VIDEO VERSION)
DIRT TRACK COWBOYS (LIVE VIDEO VERSION)
GOOD FRIENDS (LIVE VIDEO VERSION)
THE ANZAC (LIVE VIDEO VERSION)
BUILT FOR SPEED (VIDEO VERSION)
OLD HANDS (VIDEO VERSION)
THE ANZAC (VIDEO VERSION)
SHERRIF BULLFROG

GOOD FRIENDS LIVE IN CONCERT DVD
BEATING AROUND THE BUSH (LIVE VIDEO VERSION)
WHEN THE NEEDLE HITS THE VINYL (LIVE VIDEO VERSION)
GRANDPA'S PIANO (LIVE VIDEO VERSION)
YOU'RE A REVHEAD (LIVE VIDEO VERSION)
LAST MAN STANDING (LIVE VIDEO VERSION)
I DID WHAT? (LIVE VIDEO VERSION)
I STILL CALL AUSTRALIA HOME (LIVE VIDEO VERSION)
WHEN I GET MY WHEELS (LIVE VIDEO VERSION)
GOOD THINGS IN LIFE (LIVE VIDEO VERSION)
YOU ARE TO ME (LIVE VIDEO VERSION)

LITTLE SISTERS (LIVE VIDEO VERSION)
COME FROM THE HEART (LIVE VIDEO VERSION)
UNCLE PETE (LIVE VIDEO VERSION)
DIRT TRACK COWBOYS (LIVE VIDEO VERSION)
GOOD FRIENDS (LIVE VIDEO VERSION)
LAST MAN STANDING (VIDEO VERSION)
GRANDPA'S PIANO (VIDEO VERSION)
DIRT TRACK COWBOYS (VIDEO VERSION)
LOVE AWAY THE NIGHT (VIDEO VERSION)
GOOD FRIENDS (VIDEO VERSION)
BEATING AROUND THE BUSH (VIDEO VERSION)
UNCLE PETE
GOOD FRIENDS
DIRT TRACK COWBOYS
KING OF THE ROAD
BEATING AROUND THE BUSH
GOOD THINGS IN LIFE

ADAM BRAND UNSORTED LYRICS
REVHEAD LYRICS
WORDS CANNOT SAY LYRICS
TROUBLE LYRICS
MY MAMA TOLD ME (NOT TO PLAY THE GUITAR) LYRICS
LOSING STREAK LYRICS
KINDA LIKE IT LYRICS
HERE AND THERE LYRICS
COME FROM THE HEART LYRICS
DIRT TRACK COWBOYS LYRICS
GRANDPA'S PIANO LYRICS
KING OF THE ROAD LYRICS
LAST MAN STANDING LYRICS
MY MINDS MADE UP ! LYRICS
SIZE TWO BOOTS LYRICS
UNCLE PETE LYRICS
NEVER LIVE WITHOUT YOU LYRICS
LOVE AWAY THE NIGHT LYRICS

BIBLIOGRAPHY

Adam Brand picture: Courtesy Jill Stewart Austar
Communications
Adam Brand:
http://www.lyred.com/lyrics/Adam+Brand/Adam+Brand/

Blame It On Eve:
http://www.gumtreemusic.com.au/music/adam-brand/blame-it-
on-eve.aspx

Adam Brand - Blame It On Eve Limited Edition (CD AND
DVD): http://www.gumtreemusic.com.au/music/adam-
brand/blame-it-on-eve-limited-edition.aspx

Hell Of A Ride CD:
http://www.gumtreemusic.com.au/music/adam-brand/hell-of-a-
ride.aspx

Built For Speed:
http://www.lyred.com/lyrics/Adam+Brand/Built+For+Speed/

Get Loud: http://www.lyred.com/lyrics/Adam+Brand/Get+Loud/

Good Friends:
http://www.lyred.com/lyrics/Adam+Brand/Good+Friends/

What A Life (2006):
http://www.stlyrics.com/songs/a/adambrand17438.html

Adam Brand (1998):
http://www.stlyrics.com/songs/a/adambrand17438.html

Christmas In Australia (2005):
http://www.stlyrics.com/songs/a/adambrand17438.html

It's Gonna Be OK CD:
http://www.gumtreemusic.com.au/music/adam-brand/its-gonna-
be-ok.aspx

Adam Brand - Greatest Hits 1998 - 2008 CD:
http://www.gumtreemusic.com.au/music/adam-brand/greatest-
hits-1998-2008.aspx

Adam Brand - Built For Speed - Live In Concert
DVD:http://www.gumtreemusic.com.au/music/adam-
brand/built-for-speed-live.aspx

Good Friends Live In Concert DVD:
http://www.gumtreemusic.com.au/music/adam-brand/good-
friends-live-in-concert.aspx

Good Friends; Get Loud:
http://www.doubleday.com.au/Products/Music/Good+Friends+G
et+Loud+by+Adam+Brand/2917_1.aspx

Adam Brand/Built for Speed:
http://new.music.yahoo.com/adam-brand/albums/adam-brand-
built-for-speed--58236557

Adam Brand: http://gosong.net/adam_brand.html

Greatest Hits 1998-2008 DVD:
http://www.doubleday.com.au/Products/DVD/Greatest+Hits+19
98-2008+by+Adam+Brand/28675_4.aspx

Adam Brand Unsorted
Lyrics:http://www.allthelyrics.com/lyrics/adam_brand/other_son
gs_204247/

ABOUT THE AUTHOR

I was 59 years old; a mother of three very special and supportive adult children and a grandmother of three wonderful grandsons (I now have five grand-children.) when I started writing my first book whilst watching a Bon Jovi concert DVD. (I am an avid fan, if you can call me that; crazy is more like it.)

I write from the heart and I really enjoyed writing the book so I wrote another using a different artist, and the books kept coming to me and I kept writing them.(with a little help from above)

Because I use different artist/artists song titles I have to be very careful with Copyright so a lot of legal requirements have to be taken into consideration before publishing the books. I also needed a name that would connect my books to each other; so the "Song Title Series" books began.

All my books are short stories; however it depends on how many song titles there are to be used, as to the length of the book. Some artists didn't have enough song titles on their own so I combined them with a few other artists. Other artists had that many song titles that I could have written a novel; but it would have ended up being boring.

Challenges I like, so writing books with various artists are a lot of fun and require careful thinking.

Why should I have all the fun writing the books and not be able to share them with everyone; so I have converted them into large print books so that you can share my fun as well.

Hopefully in the not too distant future; the books will also be available as audio books so that no-one will miss out on my fun and enjoyment of writing these unique books. I hope that you enjoy reading them.

My web site www.songtitleseries.com is the place to visit for updates of new books and a place to purchase other titles in other formats.

TESTIMONIALS

Joan has come up with a really unique concept with this 'Song Title Series"
I found this book interesting, and was fascinated at the way she has included so many song titles into the story.
It's a great read and something a little different from most novels.
Adam Harvey (Australian Country Music Artist)

"Having read three of the Song Title Series, all in the Country Music field, I found them to be a very interesting and refreshing change to the usual books that I read.
Joan has written them very well, and has used loads of imagination and cleverness to make them very unique! Very impressive!!"
Colleen B…Tamworth (Country Music Capital)

After reading through your range of books I felt I must compliment you Joan on the imaginative and entertaining way in which you presented each group and the Musicians in those groups. The way the stories were constructed is a credit to your work ethic. These must have taken considerable time to piece together and it is obviously a work of love for you.
I wish you all the success you truly deserve and look forward to seeing you next time you visit Tamworth.
Peter Harkins   Managing Director Cheapa Music
Country Music Capital Tamworth

The song titles series are books that were intriguing and were hard to believe that these short stories were written within the incorporated song titles of the artists that are mentioned in the titles. I loved what I have read so far and think that anyone with an imagination and love of music as the author you will surely enjoy reading these.
L.K. Brisbane Australia.

Joan Maguire Books are very nice, I enjoy reading them so much, they are hard to put down!! Especially when she does one about Bonjovi and their songs!!!
If I can say, it is worth every penny, when you buy one!!! The Books make nice presents, for a person whom loves to read!!!
I can guarantee that you will LOVE these books, because I do!!!!!!!!!
Dawn from Newark, Delaware in the United States of America

I am Susie and would like to tell you guys, how much I am enjoying Joan Maguire's Books!! They are very enjoyable, and they are something that you do not ever want to put down!! I really enjoy these books; I can't wait until the next one that she puts out!!!!!!! I say go to your local book store, today and get one, you will not be disappointed!!!!!
Sue-from the United States of America